BASEBALL IMPOSTERS

THE DARK SIDE OF FANDOM

Endorsements

"Rob Sheinkopf has written a disturbingly charming book about a collection of men who claimed to have lived the baseball dream but really didn't. Many of us wanted to be ballplayers at some time in our youth, but these guys took that aspiration and transformed it into a very different kind of fantasy baseball."

– **Steve Gietschier,** *author, Baseball: The Turbulent Midcentury Years*

"Rob Sheinkopf's brilliantly reported tales of big league deceit are often hilarious, frequently shocking, but always engrossing. Once you start reading, you won't be able to stop. Nothing is more entertaining than the fanciful delusions of Baseball Imposters."

– **Jim Walker,** *Professor Emeritus, Saint Xavier University co-author, "Red Barber: The Life and Legacy of a Baseball Legend"*

"When I served as reference librarian at the National Baseball Hall of Fame, I often found myself speaking with people who had a man in their life who falsely claimed to have played professional baseball. Some were fondly remembered and keenly missed by family and friends, but oftentimes the man stood right before me with his kids, grandkids, new girlfriend, or other family members.

I always tried to be courteous and respectful as I explained that baseball is perhaps the most highly documented aspect of American life, and there was very little chance the claim was true. Sometimes this resulted in disbelief, tears, even anger. Trying to save face for the man and his family, I frequently suggested he might have played in a semipro, industrial, or municipal league, accounting for the confusion.

Rob Sheinkopf's awesome book, Baseball Imposters details many of these amazing stories in all their pathos and humor."

–**Tim Wiles,** *baseball writer/historian*

"Rob Sheinkopf has created a unique work documenting the shadowy side of baseball fandom, weaving a tapestry of engrossing, funny, and incredible stories of fraudsters, characters, and wannabes you won't find anywhere else."

– **Jon Leonoudakis,** *Documentary Filmmaker, Hano: A Century in the Bleachers*

"Baseball Imposters is a quirky, meaningful book that delves into an often overlooked side of the game. Many of us, as children, wish we could grow up to become Major Leaguers. I never would have guessed that so many people lie about imaginary baseball glory. A fun, worthwhile read."

–**Dan Good,** *author, Playing Through the Pain: Ken Caminiti and the Steroids Confession That Changed Baseball Forever*

"I would never have guessed there are so many fascinating stories in the outrageous lies and gross exaggerations some men tell – many from esteemed occupations – in claiming they had once been major-league baseball players. Equally entertaining are the culprit's reactions upon being exposed… angry denials, elaborate excuses, threats, and more.

Along the way, interesting insights into the psyche of men who feel the need to fabricate sports careers to impress others. This imposter baseball career phenomenon is common enough that there's an actual name for it: Eddie Scissons Syndrome. This book is amazing… Five stars!"

– **George Gmelch,** *Emeritus Professor of Anthropology, University of San Francisco and Union College. Author of several baseball books, including the award winning narrative, "Playing With Tigers, a minor league chronicle of the sixties"*

BASEBALL IMPOSTERS

THE DARK SIDE OF FANDOM

ROB SHEINKOPF

For Lisa and Bochy, my loving, reliable companions.
And for Molly, with advice from her Zayde…
stay away from characters like these.

And of course, this book is also dedicated to
Dr. Richard Crepeau, without whom this 40-year
research project would never have even begun.

FOREWORD

Given the right circumstances and the right person, Imagination, Memory, and Fantasy can be closely related and shape one another. Memory is not always accurate and at times is clouded and/or reshaped by Imagination and Fantasy. It is good to remember this when dealing with *The Eddie Scissions Syndrome*.

In compiling this massive list of examples of the syndrome, Rob Sheinkopf, I, and it turns out, many others, have encountered people, who for whatever reason, claim they played major league baseball. There seems to be no particular demographic shared by them, other than that they are overwhelmingly adult males who love baseball.

It is often claimed that every American boy at one time in their youth dreamed of playing major league baseball, and even starring in the sport. They entertain fantasies in which they hit the winning home run, usually a grand slam, in the bottom of the ninth inning, to win a game in the World Series. Does this make some men who never achieve this dream more vulnerable to the syndrome? Perhaps, but clearly there must be something beyond this.

It is also true that many of us embellish our role in important events in our lives. Some of this embellishment is minor, some major. And it is not confined to baseball or sports. At times we overvalue our opinions and our actions and exaggerate the importance of both. Sometimes our realities get mixed together and we come to truly believe our flawed memory.

For most of us our delusions do not go beyond the small circle in which we live our lives. But every now and then there may be a slip and our imagined reality and our fantasies slip into our public lives. There are more fantasies and syndromes than the one named for Eddie Scissions.

It is within all of these speculations that I think there is an explanation to Eddie Scissions Syndrome. I must admit I have yet to find it, at least to my satisfaction. I instead fall back on the fact that our world is replete with fantasies, both our own and those dumped continuously upon us. They, in turn, fire our imagination. If somehow all of this leads to confusion as to who we are, and scrambles our memory, I wouldn't be surprised.

For now, I will live with this explanation and let the liars off the hook.

Richard Crepeau

Fall, 2025

Table of Contents

INTRODUCTION

For most of us, the dream of playing big league baseball is a childhood fantasy that fades with time and ultimately dies when reality sets in. For me, that reality set in around age 5 or 6, when I sadly realized I probably wasn't going to be a professional baseball player. (Everyone was bigger and more athletic than I was, plus I wore thick glasses and looked like a doofus who couldn't catch or hit a ball, probably because I was a doofus who couldn't catch or hit a ball). But for a select few, that dream doesn't ever die. Instead, it morphs into an altered reality. Those select few are the grown men who, for reasons as complex as the human psyche itself, have chosen to live a lie that they played Major League Baseball.

These guys are not former major leaguers. Most never played professionally at any level. Some, not all, played high school baseball, some played college ball, others may have played minor league baseball, finishing a long way from fulfilling the dream, but they represent themselves as if they had, weaving intricate, imagined tales of baseball glory.

This book is a journey into that world, with characters suffering from a phenomenon known as "Eddie Scissons Syndrome," which sports historian Dr. Richard Crepeau in 1989 summarized as "the practice of grown men falsely claiming to have played major league baseball. It is much more common than one would think; the variety and creativity of stories told are mind-numbing."

There are still many men who shamelessly pass themselves off as former Major League Baseball players. Some have even deluded themselves into actually believing it, but most guys know they are lying and just assume they'll get away with it. And they seem to enjoy living a lie.

The name of the syndrome is inspired by a character from W.P. Kinsella's magic realism novel, *Shoeless Joe,* which served as the basis for the Kevin Costner movie, *Field of Dreams.*

In the book, Eddie Scissons claims to be the oldest living Chicago Cub, but later in the novel we discover he has been lying about his past, fooling all who knew him in his small Iowa town. While Eddie's character does not appear in *Field of Dreams,* Kinsella refers to Eddie Scissons in many of his other books and interviews, naming the syndrome after him and identifying this strange behavior.

As W.P. Kinsella—channeling the character of Ray—wrote about Eddie:

"I remember my own indignation after I discovered Eddie's secret. After I'd talked to him on the street in Iowa City that windy March afternoon, I had hustled off to the nearby Iowa City Public Library to find a copy of the Baseball Encyclopedia and check out Eddie's statistics. I'd had an uneasy feeling that something was not right, for he had spoken of playing in Wrigley Field in 1908, '09, and '10, and I knew without looking it up that that was at least five years before Wrigley Field was built, and that in those years the Cubs would have played in West Side Park. ... I remember the disappointment and

then the anger I felt as I found that no one named Scissons had ever pitched in the major leagues. I tried the Player Register, in case I had misunderstood about his being a pitcher. But I also drew a blank there. For whatever reason, Eddie Scissons had been lying to me."

The Beginning of my Journey

I personally experienced Eddie Scissons Syndrome for the first time (that I know of) in 1985 and have spent the ensuing four decades uncovering—and in some cases, calling out—true-life **Baseball Imposters**. Unlike Ray, I have not usually avoided the difficult conversations or brushed aside the truth. Looking back, there were times I probably should have.

After exploring and researching this curious affliction for all these years, I finally decided to write a book about it. I'm 74 years old now as this book is released, and I don't want my research into Eddie Scissons Syndrome to die with me. I want it to carry forward, honoring the 23,000-plus players who actually made it to the big leagues, not the pretenders, phonies and con artists trying to capitalize on someone else's glory. I want this book to honor the hard work and dedication, the sacrifices made and the on-field accomplishments of these 23,000-plus men (yes, someday we will be able to say, "men and women", but for now, these "men") and not allow baseball imposters to tarnish their attainment of reaching the highest professional level, being recognized as the very best in their field.

This phenomenon is similar to the concept of "stolen valor" and lying about military qualifications or accomplishments. In some cases, stolen valor is punishable by law. (I think Eddie Scissons Syndrome should be as well). Stolen Valor brings up a myriad of complex emotions, some of which are similar to Eddie Scissons Syndrome. Nathan Webster, noted photojournalist who served in Operation Desert Storm, wrote about a friend who took credit for military accomplishments that were not his own.

"Toward my friend, I felt—feel—embarrassed," Webster wrote about his friend's stolen valor. "Whatever gets you through the day, but I don't want to know about it. In this squeezing, grasping era, stolen valor seems so grubby – stolen for what? To impress who?"[1] Webster confronted his friend through email, upon reading he claimed to have been awarded a purple heart. He wrote, "Purple heart? Not cool, dude." He expected and received no reply. "I wanted him to feel that shiver up the spine we all feel, that I've felt, when our awkward lies are revealed." Webster's comments are applicable to ESS as they are to Stolen Valor.

This book explores the elaborate and often unimaginable lies spun by men who, for various and often complex reasons, pass themselves off as former major league baseball players. It is a deep dive into the stories of these men, their motivations, and the often humorous, sometimes sad, but always fascinating details of their deceptions.

Long before Google, when this *little research project* of mine began, the only way to fact-check a claim was to do exactly what Ray did in *Shoeless Joe*, to dig up a copy of *The Baseball Encyclopedia*. Nowadays, despite instant access to online databases like Baseball Reference.com, Baseball Cube, and Retro Sheet, the scourge of this syndrome surprisingly still runs rampant.

Over the years, I've collected hundreds of examples of seemingly normal guys lying about having played major league baseball. My personal collection includes pretenders from cab drivers to physical therapists, dentists and physicians, from retail store

---

[1] Webster, Nathan. "Stolen Valor Damages Veteran Friendships & Reputations." The War Horse, thewarhorse.org/stolen-valor-damages-veteran-friendships-reputations/.

clerks to parents of students I encountered on my job, from local political candidates not named George Santos to spouses of colleagues, from job applicants (and college admissions applicants) to former and current neighbors. I've even crossed paths with a chiropractor who wore a World Series ring, displayed pictures of himself in full Yankee uniform in the lobby of his office, and told his patients he played in the World Series for the New York Yankees. In this book, you'll read about my confrontation with that chiropractor, and his ultimate justification for the charade.

The stories I share here are based upon *lies*. Lies told to me, lies told to many people who shared their experiences of being lied to, lies that were exposed and became high profile news items, lies that appeared in obituaries and in some cases only uncovered by unwitting, grief-stricken families after the death of a loved one, and much more. The underlying reasons people lie about having played major league baseball are complicated and at the same time easy to understand.

This fantasy of playing professional baseball begins when we're very young, and it is hard to shake. Some people can't let it go, and over time, in their own mind, the fantasy becomes a false reality, and with the retelling of the lie—over and over to different audiences, to work colleagues and new friends, to new acquaintances at parties, to passengers in their Uber, in a line at the grocery store, on an airplane with a captive audience in the adjoining seat, and for the boldest (and most shameful) of liars, at a lectern on a Sunday morning, entertaining fellow church-goers about life lessons (never) learned on the baseball diamond—the lie becomes their reality, a personal history for the storyteller. In many cases, they actually come to believe they played in the major leagues! It is not uncommon to hear stunning details of game situations, conversations with teammates and managers (that never happened), batting averages and other statistics that were never compiled, and painful details from game situations that never were, from those who never played, but became afflicted with Eddie Scissons Syndrome.

While it's not difficult to understand how someone could fall victim to the Syndrome, I am still troubled by it and feel there's something not quite right about a guy lying about having played in the Big Leagues. Does he deserve our compassion? I don't think so, but I know some people who don't feel the same way, and I understand if you disagree.

It used to be pretty easy to get away with claiming you played minor league baseball, not so much anymore with Baseball Reference. com. But having played in the Big Leagues? That was kind of risky even 40 or 50 years ago with the Big Mac. These days, especially with the Internet and modern technology supporting researchers like you and me, it doesn't take much to catch someone in the lie, so if you think the Syndrome is a thing of the past, you'd be wrong.

Eddie Scissons Syndrome is rampant. I know. I've studied it since 1985. It's not going away despite modern technology that should have embarrassed sufferers into submission.

While a guy's story checks out every now and then, the rule—not the exception—is a made-up story with a tremendous amount of detail added to make it seem real. Some of the examples presented here are modern day and easily proven to be false. Some are from the pre-Internet era but still relevant and hard to pass up for their entertainment and value to our story.

I should tell you, that in the spirit of full transparency, and with the advice of legal counsel, I have changed the names of many of my (thus unrevealed) subjects to avoid being sued for defamation of character and to avoid taking a beating from any guy clever enough to Google himself and somehow discover my research, revealing his real name associated with his non-existent and now exposed fake-baseball career. Look, these guys deserve to be exposed for their lies, no question about it, but not necessarily by me and not necessarily in a court of law… and certainly not necessarily if there is any chance of finding me in a pool of blood after trying to justify why their name appeared in my book.

It's been quite an adventure…disappointing, embarrassing and sad to uncover lies, and for whatever reason, I've felt a need to explore and reveal them. In the early stages of my research, I truly hoped that exposing these bad apples might deter others. But over the years, the number of bad apples appear to be growing, or maybe we're just getting better at spotting the liars.

I hope that this book will help you keep from being fooled by Eddie Scissons Syndrome yourself. Who knows, maybe wider awareness of the syndrome will deter other wannabe players from making grandiose, false claims.

Almost every time I speak to groups about this topic, and I have done so dozens of times over the years, I hear from people who have their own stories to tell about someone they met who passed himself off as a former Major League Baseball player. It never fails. And it's usually someone you'd never suspect, like the character in Kinsella's book.

If you have an Eddie Scissons Syndrome encounter you'd like to share on my blog, or if you're interested in booking me for a speaking engagement or interview, please visit my website, **Robsheinkopf-Author.com**. I'm always happy to talk about this topic with anyone willing to listen, (and hopefully inspire you to share *your* story!)

By shining a light on these *Baseball Imposters*, I hope to not only expose them but also to better understand what makes us so willing to believe them in the first place. This book is a testament to the enduring power of the baseball dream and the lengths some men will go through to live it, even if only in their own minds.

Rob Sheinkopf

Fall, 2025

Chapter 1

THE BEGINNING
OF A LONG JOURNEY

My journey began in 1985, when I wrote a master's thesis that investigated what former Major League Baseball (MLB) players did after retiring from baseball, what second careers they pursued, and how they prepared for the huge lifestyle changes they were about to experience. Back then, very few ballplayers made enough money during their baseball careers to be able to simply stop working when it came time to call it quits, so the question regarding vocational choices had relevance. Obviously, times have changed, and second-career decision-making is not as critical an issue for today's major leaguers.

The average salary for a player in 1975, for example, was $44,676, and the minimum salary was only $16,000. That translates in 2025 money to an average of almost $250,000, and a minimum of just over $88,000. When you consider that in 2023 the average salary was more than $4.4 million with a minimum of more than $720,000, rising to $780,000 by 2026, these guys have done pretty well for themselves. And I suspect that by the time you read this book, they will be doing even better.

My master's thesis was titled *An Analysis of Factors Influencing Second Career Decision-Making Among Retired Major League Baseball Players Prior to Free Agency.* It was a case-study approach that involved 53 personal interviews with MLB retirees, some obscure, some well-known, but all were former major leaguers.

As I was to discover, all but one, that is.

My wife bought me a wonderful graduation gift, a shiny new copy of the 3,200-page, 1985 edition of *The Baseball Encyclopedia.* One rainy day I decided to look up each of my subjects, just for fun. And it *was* fun… until I discovered that Joseph Edward Cavallo was not in the book.

Joe owned the J.E. Cavallo Insurance Agency in Orlando, Florida, and because of his generous support of University of Central Florida athletics, he had the honor of throwing out the first pitch at a baseball game once a year. Joe tipped his Chief Wahoo cap to the crowd, which just learned from the P.A. announcer that Joe was the Cleveland Indians' starting shortstop in 1978, playing in 151 games and hitting .277 with 13 home runs. He signed autographs and posed for pictures with fans as he strolled through the ballpark. He basked in his celebrity status, generously giving his time and attention to adoring fans, many of whom had never seen a major league player up close like that. They didn't know as they walked off with a signed ball that they still hadn't.

During our long conversation, Joe revealed he never played minor league ball. Instead, he went straight to the Big Leagues right after his junior year of college! While not impossible, that should have been a red flag.

The house fire

I guess Joe figured no one followed the Cleveland Indians back then because, really, no one did. They were horrible, year after year. I suspect most people who lived in Cleveland in the late '70s wouldn't even question Joe's story. And when asked about pictures or memorabilia he might share with me as I wrote my chapter about him, he told me the sad tale of a house fire that destroyed everything. And I should point out that as my research unfolded, I was to discover that housefires are pretty commonplace among retired Major League Baseball players… or more accurately, among those *lying* about having played Major League Baseball.

Joe's ankle injury—the one he supposedly suffered on the last day of the 1978 season trying to steal home, which he claimed would have won the game for Cleveland and sent them to the postseason[2]—never quite healed properly, so he retired from baseball and began a lucrative career selling life insurance, passing himself off as a former professional baseball player. His advertising and marketing campaigns all not so subtly referred to his MLB experience, and I'm sure prospective customers were entertained with personal anecdotes and exciting game summaries that existed only in Mr. Cavallo's mind, not in any box score on record.

Chasing the truth

Joe spent four or five hours answering my questions and relating some painfully detailed personal anecdotes about his baseball career… how he still had some coursework to complete the requirements for his bachelor's degree when he joined the Indians, and how he would hide his textbooks behind comic books on plane rides so his teammates wouldn't ridicule him for studying calculus or organic chemistry… or reading poetry.

Maybe I should have caught on then. I mean, who reads poetry?

Joe didn't care that now five pages of my master's thesis are

---

[2] Joe should have double-checked his facts—Cleveland was a last place team, finishing 69-90 that year.

based upon his lies. The level of detail he shared with me about his non-existent baseball career was *stunning*.

Given the effort he had made and the lengths he had gone to in sharing his stories with me, I wanted to devote the same amount of effort in properly exploring his account before calling him a liar. Maybe there was some other explanation. Maybe there was something I overlooked.

So, I called Western Kentucky University and their head baseball coach, who would have been there during the years Joe claimed to have played for the team, *never heard of him!* Remember, Joe was a guy who jumped from WKU, division-one college athletics but certainly not known as a baseball powerhouse. A guy like Joe would have stood out to the WKU coaching staff, as well as the rest of the college baseball loving country. I also called the coach of his high school alma mater in Owensboro, Kentucky. They had a new coach since Joe had graduated, and he offered to do some research and report back. A few days later, he called back as promised, and the athletic department's records revealed that Joe Cavallo had tried out for his high school team but was not selected. His name appeared on a tryout list—kept for insurance purposes—but he did not appear on player rosters for any of his high school years. He never made the team!

I was pretty angry and embarrassed for falling for it, and I needed to confront Joe. I needed to hear his explanation. Several pages of my master's thesis were now fraudulent, and I felt it was my fault. I should have checked this guy out, I should have doubted his story. But back then, I had no reason to doubt a guy like Joe, whom I admired… after all, he was a celebrity throughout the Orlando community, and no one else seemed to doubt him. Why should I?

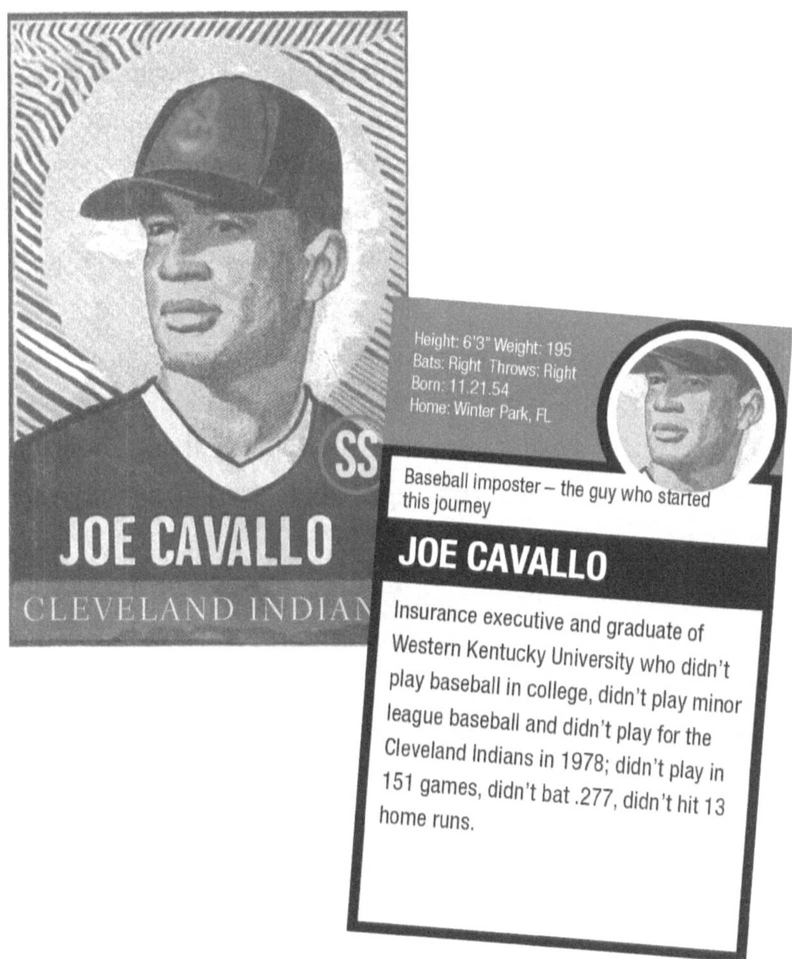
JOE CAVALLO
CLEVELAND INDIAN
SS
Height: 6'3" Weight: 195
Bats: Right Throws: Right
Born: 11.21.54
Home: Winter Park, FL
Baseball imposter — the guy who started this journey
JOE CAVALLO
Insurance executive and graduate of Western Kentucky University who didn't play baseball in college, didn't play minor league baseball and didn't play for the Cleveland Indians in 1978; didn't play in 151 games, didn't bat .277, didn't hit 13 home runs.

The confrontation

In fall 1985, shortly after these revelations came to light, Joe and I were among guests in the President's suite at a UCF football game. I was there as the Director of Admissions, entertaining high school principals and guidance counselors, and recruiting students. He was there with his family as an athletic booster, supporting UCF athletics, and hopefully mingling with potential insurance clients. I saw him signing a baseball for a guest in the suite, and waited for my turn, confronting him during halftime at a buffet table after the line had thinned out and when no one else was around. I got his attention and politely asked him why he fed me a pack of elaborate lies.

After a long, uncomfortable silence, Joe nervously pretended that he didn't know what I was talking about, and as he walked away, he said, "I'll call you next week, Rob. We'll talk about it." He never did, and not surprisingly, he never returned my calls after that.

For my thesis, I interviewed Andy Seminick, George Mercury Myatt, Jack Billingham, George Susce, Jim Lyttle, Dave Giusti, Bob Buhl, Wonderful Willie Smith, and about forty-five other guys, including Joe Cavallo. I had to look up some of the others in the Big Mac, as many played in the '30s and '40s, even before *my* time. But Joe Cavallo? C'mon, he was a well-known business leader and everyone in Orlando knew he played Major League Baseball just a few years ago! He was the shortstop for the Cleveland Indians! Everyone knew that, but me… and MacMillan Publishing.

It was embarrassing for me to unravel Joe's lies and recognize how I'd fallen for them.

I wanted to believe him—so much so, that I let his lies go unchecked. Part of the problem was the mystique of being a Major League Baseball player. The players are living out a boyhood dream, and even the worst players in the league are still among the best players in the world. The fifth outfielder, the innings-eating middle reliever, the back-up catcher, and the player who only got a quick cup of coffee in the show playing an inning or two before being dispatched to Nowhereville in the minor leagues, never to return, *still made it.* They are forever major leaguers. And I spent hours talking to … some guy who hadn't played Major League Baseball. He hadn't played minor league baseball either, hadn't played in college or in high school. I'd interviewed a fraud, and I wrote down every word he said. I thought he was the only one, or at least part of a small band of outlaws, Liars! Turns out, he was in good (by that I mean bad) company, that there was a full roster of guys whose greatest baseball exploits occurred in their own minds. And now that I was aware of the charade, it seemed like new examples kept popping up with regularity.

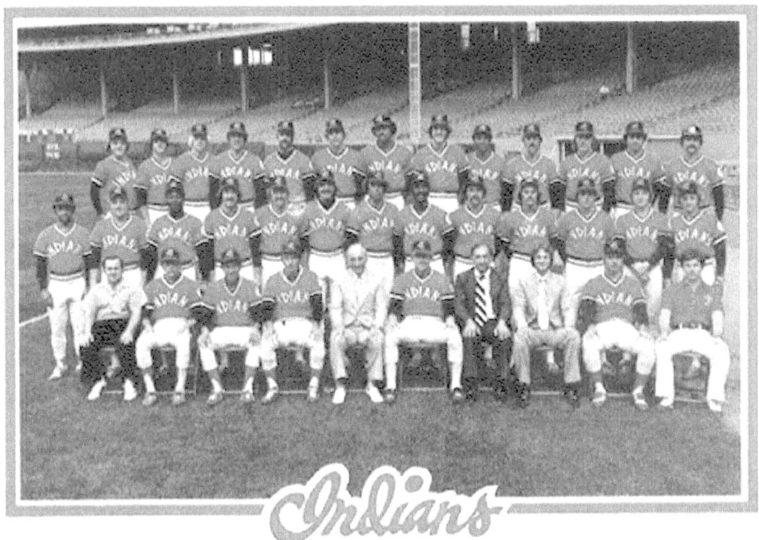

"Do you see Joe Cavallo in this picture of the 1978 Cleveland Indians?
No, you don't."

Chapter 2

THE "BIG MAC"

My experience with Joe Cavallo, who was definitely *not* a major leaguer, led me down a very long rabbit hole. Back in the 1980s, there was no Internet, no Google, no Base-ball-Reference.com, no *anything* dot com…only *The Baseball Encyclopedia*, known as the "Big Mac," (*not so coincidentally* published by Macmillan & Company).

The Big Mac includes every player who ever played major league baseball since 1876, and it was our only reliable source to fact check a story and determine the credibility of a claim that the storyteller indeed played major league baseball.

The Big Mac

If a player's name is not in the Big Mac, there's a 100% chance he never played major league baseball. And as far as confirming that someone had played *minor* league baseball, well, that was next to impossible back when I began my research.

You may remember Archibald "Moonlight" Graham, whom we got to meet from his appearance in *Field of Dreams*. He is in the *Baseball Encyclopedia*. The real-life "Moonlight" Graham actually played right field for the New York Giants for one inning in 1905 but never came to bat. He's in the book.

Archibald "Moonlight" Graham

So is Ray Kennedy, a 21-year-old catcher whose only appearance in the Big Leagues was as a pinch hitter for the St. Louis Browns in the eighth inning of a game on September 8, 1916, against the Detroit Tigers. After hitting a soft ground ball to the second baseman for a routine out, Ray's manager, Fielder Jones, called him over, handed him the lineup card and supposedly said, "Hey, kid, here's a souvenir. Now go out and get a real job," according to my friend Milly Kennedy, Ray's 98-year-old daughter who still has that framed lineup card displayed in her home. His brief playing career ended shortly thereafter when he was released at the close of the 1916 season.

Ray Kennedy took his manager's advice, embarking on a remarkable 53-year career as a general manager, player personnel director, minor league coordinator, and scout for the New York Yankees, the Pittsburgh Pirates, Detroit Tigers, Philadelphia Athletics, and the New York Mets until his death in 1969. Kennedy is in the Big Mac for his one and only appearance as a pinch hitter on September 8, 1916, *not* for his long, successful career in baseball's front office.

Ray Kennedy (top). Milly Kennedy and her father's lineup card from 9.8.1916

And then there's Larry Yount, older brother of Hall of Famer Robin Yount, who sadly, in his only major league appearance on September 15, 1971, had to leave the game while still throwing warm-up pitches due to injury, and never faced a big league batter then or at any time in the future. Larry Yount is in the Big Mac because he *entered* a major league game, even though he never actually faced a batter.

Today you don't have to cart around the 3,000+ page Big Mac to prove a lie like in the old days. Modern technology enables you to take out your phone in front of the former Big Leaguer and verify his story instantly, or more likely, humiliate the liar … and please do it publicly (keep reading for my own tips for addressing people you suspect of lying). With the new technology, you might think the Syndrome would be old news, like talking about Bubonic Plague or Polio, or Smallpox. Sadly, that just is not the case. The new technology apparently hasn't scared the liars into submission… to them, it's more like a bad cold.

Yes, times have changed, but Eddie Scissons Syndrome lingers on, just as current and timeless as it was when an obscure writer named Kinsella started penning stories about an Iowa farmer, building a baseball field in his cornfield.

Chapter 3

WHO DOESN'T REMEMBER HIS PITCHING COACH?

I was devastated when I discovered Joe Cavallo's lie.

I took this slight personally. He lied to *me!* For my master's thesis! Did I alert the dean of the department and ask if I should redo my thesis? No. Instead, I brought it to someone else's attention—my friend, Professor Dick Crepeau.

Dick was, and is, one of the country's most preeminent baseball historians. He authored the book *Baseball: America's Diamond Mind, 1919-1941* and has written a bounty of journal essays and presented hundreds of academic papers. And apparently having written two authorized editions of the *History of the NFL* didn't diminish his baseball reputation.

"Has this ever happened to you?" I asked him after telling him of the revelation of Joe Cavallo's big lie and the now compromised master's degree.

"Not that I know of." was his response, and I suspect Dick felt a sense of relief that my degree wasn't in his department, and really someone else's problem. I contacted my thesis advisor, who assured me the thesis need not be redone and my degree was valid, despite one of my subjects being a fraud. That was a relief.

Dick and I both shook our heads, there wasn't much we could do about it now. And then, a few weeks later, a guy I met who worked for a sign company in Orlando told me he'd pitched for the Braves in the 1970s.

"Oh, you played with Dale Murphy and Biff Pocoroba?" I asked him, naming some other more memorable names from the Atlanta's teams he supposedly played with. He said he had.

Not long after that, a friend of mine who *did* play for the Tigers, Bryan Kelly, got a job at the same sign company, and I told Bryan about his colleague's experience pitching for Atlanta. Soon after, I met up with Bryan and asked about his colleague at work.

"Hey, did you connect with that guy?" I asked him.

"He's a liar," Bryan told me. "He didn't play for the Braves."

"Why do you say that?"

"Because I asked him a few questions and he didn't know anything. I said, 'who was your pitching coach?' And he said, 'I don't know.'" (*How quickly one forgets Herm Starrette and Johnny Sain and Cloyd Boyer…*). Bryan went on to tell me he remembers every pitching coach he has had since Little League. "There's no way he played in the Big leagues."

These incidents— Joe Cavallo and this wannabe Braves pitcher—happened back to back within just a few days. I brought it up to Crepeau the next time I saw him, and after brief conversations about Rod Serling and the possibility that we were in fact in an alternate universe of some kind, we agreed something had to be done.

"Robby, you've got to read Kinsella." Kinsella as in W.P. "Bill" Kinsella, the eccentric and talented baseball author. Dick convinced me to expand my baseball horizons, maybe do some reading and actually learn something. So, I went out and bought a couple of Kinsella's books. One of those books was *Shoeless Joe,* the basis for the movie, *Field of Dreams.* All of Kinsella's books were terrific, well worth reading, but *Shoeless Joe…* that one turned out to be well worth turning into a movie. And we all know movies are way better than books! As usual, Professor Crepeau pointed me in the right direction.

W.P. Kinsella

In his writing, Kinsella often referred to this character Eddie Scissons, who claimed to be the oldest living Chicago Cub —but in actuality, he hadn't played Major League Baseball at all. Kinsella's writing inspired me, and having had these recent, personal experiences, I finally understood why there was a name for this thing: *Eddie Scissons Syndrome.*

This thing was real. I was to find out the Joe Cavallos of this world were a lot more common than I'd anticipated. With my radar attuned, these encounters now seemed to happen frequently. And I started keeping track and making notes.

Chapter 4

TRANSCRIPTS, TEST SCORES, AND LIES

During my 40-year career in higher education, much of it spent at the University of Central Florida, I crossed paths with lots of people throughout the university and had especially deep connections with the athletic department. If coaches were trying to land a star recruit, for example, they'd work with me to ensure that the athlete had at least met NCAA minimums before taking the case further to convince a faculty committee. My job was uniquely focused on official transcripts and test scores, verifiable qualifications with personal statements to fill in the gaps where objective data fell short.

So, this business of guys randomly lying about playing a sport that is so well documented, where statisticians and writers earn their living by keeping track of everything… it amused and fascinated me. At first, I almost couldn't believe this was really a thing until I couldn't deny it was a thing anymore. How could people possibly think no one would find out they are lying? Or did they just not care if they were found out?

He just forgot to mention it before…

I always displayed my baseball memorabilia in my office (since my wife would never allow it in our home). Entering a director of admissions office that looks like it should be the baseball coach's office seemed to encourage people to discuss their love of baseball, and frequently the conversation led to stories just too good to be true.

I always took notes and had *The Baseball Encyclopedia* on full display, consulting it on an as-needed basis. And it was *needed* pretty often. I was uniquely positioned to hear—and prove or disprove—all of these detailed stories of baseball glory, most of which turned out to be false.

That was the case with Jack McEndry, whom I'd known for years. He, like everyone who has ever met me, knew I am a die-hard baseball fan, yet he never mentioned having played for manager Ted Williams and the Washington Senators back in the day. Must have just slipped his mind, I guess.

Until one night when he blurted out among a group of my friends at the UCF-Florida State baseball game, "the game has changed so much since I played." Then the conversation took a dark turn when one of my friends asked him playfully for whom he played. Along with playing for Teddy Ballgame and the Senators, he proclaimed his favorite teammate was Frank Howard (who liked to call his little buddy "Jackie"), and he described his elation celebrating on the field after he and his teammates on the 1965 Twins won the American League pennant, even though "I went 0–4 that day".

I guess my friend Jack must have just forgotten to mention it before, you know the *hundreds* of times we saw each other on campus over the years and the many conversations we had, watching dozens of UCF games together … and yes, by now you probably guessed that the Big Mac forgot to include Jack McEndry. But this one hurt, as I thought we were friends, and why would a friend lie like that to a friend? It didn't make any sense. I never did confront Jack, it was just too painful, but I did avoid being around him from that point forward.

Oh, it wouldn't be in *that* book…

Another early example of ESS occurred when I was interviewing a student who had been academically disqualified the previous semester. He asked for a chance to petition for a second chance and be readmitted on probation.

This guy, upon entering my office, commented on my baseball memorabilia and proclaimed that his father had played for the Dodgers. Since I always had *The Baseball Encyclopedia* in my office sitting on a dictionary stand, open and ready for just such an occasion, I thought, "Here we go again…," and checked out his story in front of him. I told him if his father *had* played, if his father's name *was* in the Big Mac, I would readmit him on probation without further conversation, knowing full well the integrity of our admissions process was not in jeopardy.

Sadly, Jimmy Van Werner's name didn't appear as a pitcher or as a position player. After making sure we had the correct spelling of his father's name, I told Junior that his dad (that is, if he was even really his dad!) never played Major League Baseball for the Dodgers or for anyone else, for that matter. Never!

Jimmy wasn't convinced. He seemed to go through all the stages of a Syndrome sufferer being caught in the act, stages that I had begun to identify from personal experience dealing with guys like Van Werner. As I looked for a way to save myself from a punch in the face, (he was in the Anger Stage), and to save Jimmy from further embarrassment, that's when he blurted out, "Well, it probably wouldn't be in *that* book because, you see, he played for the *Brooklyn* Dodgers, not the *Los Angeles* Dodgers!" I thought, oh, yea, good point, Junior.

Jimmy was not readmitted.

Chapter 5

YOU WORK FOR GRAIG NETTLES?

One of the great benefits of working at the University of Central Florida was being able to take a class, tuition-free, every semester. I took full advantage of that benefit and attended random classes for years. In the late 1980s, I signed up for my friend Dick Crepeau's Baseball History class, which was anything but random. Conversations with classmates as well as the lectures and guest speakers were fascinating, and the class was definitely worth the tuition.

Through the class I met some fellow baseball enthusiasts, including a guy who told me his boss played third base for the New York Yankees in the late 1970s.

"You work for Graig Nettles?" I asked with great excitement.

"No," he replied. "I work for Bill Tischler. He's a chiropractor, he played in the World Series for the Yankees in 1978. Dr. Tischler was the Yankees starting third baseman for several years and retired from baseball to go back to school to become a chiropractor. There's pictures of him all over our office in his Yankee uniform and everything! He even wears his World Series ring to work...

It's from 1978 when they beat the Dodgers."

Hmph. I gotta see this!

Knowing the 1970s Yankees as well as I did, I immediately knew this story was bogus, and I called Dr. Tischler's office to talk about his fake baseball career. His secretary said he was too busy to see me and he didn't want to talk about it. So, I waited a few minutes and called back, making an appointment as if I were interested in becoming a patient. They offered a special, first visit free so they could assess my chiropractic needs, then sell me on regular visits. The scams from this guy just never end! I said, "Perfect! Sign me up." I made an appointment with Dr. Tischler. I couldn't wait for my visit with the doctor so we could discuss his lies.

The office photos were *stunning*. They included two professionally produced, beautifully framed posters of Tischler in pinstripes swinging for the fences. Several smaller pictures showed him taking ground balls in the infield. Other framed photos showed him standing next to Yankees icons Roy White and Mel Stottlemyre.

They looked to me like he had attended a Yankees Fantasy Camp, and this elaborate charade took on a life of its own. (Spoiler alert!). I was to find out that's *exactly* what happened.

When it was my turn to see the doctor, my name was called and the receptionist escorted me to an examining room down the hall. I was instructed to remove my clothes and put on a patient gown. I didn't follow her orders. I wasn't *really* going to be a patient—I was there to ask questions. Plus, I hate those gowns, even when my doctor appointments are legit.

The doctor entered a few minutes later, visibly annoyed I was still in my street clothes. So, I confronted him right away so he could be angry at me for reasons other than not following his nurse's orders. Things got heated up quickly.

"How dare you come into my office and accuse me of lying," he said, flashing his World Series ring. "Who do you think you are?" Good question, but this was not about me.

He thought *that* would set me straight. It didn't. Anyone could buy a World Series ring or have one commissioned … the ring itself didn't prove anything. The Yankees were the most storied and successful franchise in baseball history, and Nettles had manned the hot corner for the team from 1973 through the early 80's, earning six All-Star selections, two Gold Glove awards and two World Series championships. Graig Nettles was no Joe Cavallo, he played on championship teams and was a high-profile star on those teams, a big reason why those teams were so successful. Graig Nettles was a well-known celebrity, maybe assuming his identity instead of that from a bench warmer on that Yankee team wasn't the smartest thing the doctor could have done.

The obvious truth? Dr. Tischler never played pro baseball, let alone Major League Baseball, never played third base for the Yankees, and never played in a World Series, and anybody who knew anything about baseball would know he was lying. In fact, just spend five minutes with this character and that would be enough to convince you he was lying about something.

"Did you *legally* change your name from Graig Nettles to William Tischler?" I finally asked him. My sarcasm and badgering finally wore him down, and he unhappily relented, admitting that he did in fact attend a Yankees fantasy camp, and that's where the idea came to him to pass himself off as a former professional ballplayer. See? Watching every Columbo episode ever made paid off. "There's just one more thing, Dr. Tischler, are you actually a real chiropractor?" No, I didn't have the nerve to actually ask him that, but it did cross my mind.

Height: 6'1" Weight: 180
Bats: Left Throws: Right
Born: 01.23.57
Home: Detroit, MI

Baseball imposter and chiropractic liar

BILL TISCHLER

Didn't play third base for the New York Yankees in 1977 and 1978, didn't play in the World Series, but he *does* proudly wear a World Series ring ... and he *did* attend Yankee Fantasy camp and he proudly displays his picture taken with former Yankee, Roy White. Dr. Tischler is not a role model ... and who knows, he may not even be a doctor.

"It's good for my business," he told me without any remorse. "It's an acceptable marketing tactic. Lots of people do that. I've done nothing wrong. My patients want a doctor who is athletic, physically fit, and a role model." The sad thing? He could have been all of these things without trying to pass himself off as a former New York Yankee.

Admitting to this elaborate fraud didn't seem to pain him in any way. It just annoyed him that he got caught. He felt justified and told me he owed no one an apology, certainly not me. The way he saw it, if his patients chose to believe he played for the Yankees, that was up to them.

I couldn't hide my disdain.

"You, sir, are no role model. You are a fraud and you should be ashamed of yourself!"

No more words were exchanged as I left the premises.

Chapter 6

ANOTHER DAY, ANOTHER YANKEE, ANOTHER BACK-UP CATCHER

After having a local artist's signed drawing of Sparky Anderson professionally framed at a shop in Orlando, I learned that the frame shop owner was a former New York Yankees player himself. *Another former Yankee! They're everywhere!* Mike Parsons told me he had also played for Coach Jay Bergman at the University of Florida. Upon graduating, Mike said he left Gainesville, signed with the Yankees and moved to Fort Lauderdale. He had a short stint in Nashville with the Sounds, in Columbus with the Clippers, and then with the New York Yankees. He apparently knew their farm system, lending to his credibility. But I knew their farm system as well, does that make me a former Yankee?

Being a knowledgeable, rabid Yankee fan, I quizzed this guy. "How come I never heard of you?"

"Well, I was a backup catcher and only played a half a season in New York. I only batted about a hundred times, hit .220 or so, with about five or six home runs. Most of my best years were in Triple-A."

MIKE
PARSONS back-up catche
Height: 5'8" Weight: 178
Bats: Right Throws: Right
Born: 05.17.69
Home: Tampa, FL
Liar and baseball imposter
MIKE PARSONS
Business owner who wasn't a back-up catcher for the New York Yankees, didn't hit "around .220", didn't hit "5 or 6 home runs", and didn't play for Coach Jay Bergman at the University of Florida. Anyone who ever really played, knows those stats, without having to guess.

There's so much wrong with that response. Guys who actually did play a half of a season with the New York Yankees know exactly how many times they came to bat, exactly what their batting average was, and exactly how many home runs they hit, not *five or six*.

Upon checking all the reference materials available to most humans, Parsons' name wasn't listed anywhere. He not only never played for the Yankees, but he also never played for the Nashville Sounds, Columbus Clippers, or any minor league team. Never!

I called my longtime friend, retired college baseball coach, Jay Bergman. And I asked him about Mike Parsons, "Who? No, Robby, never heard of the guy. He might be another one of those Eddie Jaspers you write about." Sigh. Jay couldn't recall ever recruiting, coaching or hearing the name, Mike Parsons. And if you know Jay, you know he remembers every player he ever coached and recruited over the past sixty or so years.

That beautiful drawing of Sparky Anderson hangs in my office now, and when I look at it I am often reminded of the great job Mike Parsons does, framing artwork so professionally. He should be applauded for his workmanship. Mike Parsons is a liar when it comes to baseball, but I recommend him highly if you need something framed. He'll frame it with integrity.

The details were always different, but the situation kept happening again and again. Once I saw Eddie Scissons Syndrome in a guy, I couldn't unsee it. It's like that arrow in the FedEx logo, you can't unsee it once you've recognized it.

I finally convinced Crepeau I had something, but what exactly? I had stories … but what could I do with them? I had no idea how to approach an organization about this topic or write a paper about it. But Dick had written hundreds of academic papers, his book, *Baseball, America's Diamond Mind* has been quoted by baseball historians and others for generations, and he is a widely respected sports historian. If he thinks I got something, well, that's good enough for me. Dick encouraged me to pursue this *body of knowledge* and write up this collection of cases. Recognizing he was dealing with a rookie, Dick volunteered to co-author our first paper on the topic together and guide me through the process to have it accepted at the annual SLA conference, a process that ultimately led to another connection who inspired this effort.

Chapter 7

GO THE DISTANCE

After a few years of collecting stories, it was finally time to find an audience that might be interested in hearing our story. We submitted our paper to the Sport Literature Association, and miraculously, it was accepted. Dick and I were headed to Florence, Oregon to present our findings to the SLA annual conference in 1990.

Among presenters were noted author Ken Kesey as well as a couple of other luminaries I had never heard of. But W.P. "Bill" Kinsella was on the program, reading some of his poetry and short stories. The author of *Shoeless Joe,* Kinsella had recently become a well-known figure after the movie it inspired, *Field of Dreams,* was released the previous year. His celebrity would grow because of the unexpected tremendous success of the movie, and an almost cult-like following that he would attract for his body of work. (I admit to being one of his many cult followers).

Crepeau and I were presenting our paper the same morning as Kinsella's poetry reading. Maybe a little intimidating, but we had some time after his presentation. Just before it was our turn to present our paper, titled "The Eddie Scissions Syndrome: Life

Imitating Art Imitating Life," a well-respected professor in the field of Sport Literature gave his paper on Hollywood's relationship with sport literature. Dr. Chris Messenger from the University of Illinois Chicago gave an informative and entertaining retrospective of the many Babe Ruth movies which all seemed to fall short in terms of cinematic quality because of some obvious problems with historical inaccuracy. He also discussed the recently released *Field of Dreams*, pointing out how the movie itself lacked many historical truths, (like Ray Liotta hitting from the left side, the players of that era wearing double-knit uniforms, among many others). His paper kept our interest, having so many valid points we have all noticed as movie-goers and baseball fans, and ended on a positive, complimentary (to Kinsella) note, saying that Hollywood ruins great literature. Praising *Shoeless Joe* as "great literature," Chris left the stage to thunderous applause and a reasonable expectation that the Q/A discussion period to follow would elicit nothing but high praise. It should have.

We were next, and while I was cautiously optimistic, my palms were sweating. And we certainly could not have foreseen what came next. Wrapping up Chris's paper, the moderator asked, "Mr. Kinsella, would you care to make a comment on Professor Messenger's presentation?" Having praised Kinsella for his wonderful novels, including the one that Hollywood just turned into a very popular movie, Chris had every reason to expect a positive reaction from Kinsella.

Kinsella stood slowly and spoke quietly. After a couple of questions for Chris to set the stage, he told the professor he felt sorry for him, and for his students. "You've missed the point of my *mediocre* book. It wasn't about *double-knit uniforms*, or whether or not players left their gloves on the field after an inning. I never knew if Joe Jackson batted right or left-handed and didn't care which way Ray Liotta batted". He paused, "I did care that Archie Graham gave up his baseball career in order to practice medicine (and save the child from choking on a hot dog), and that Terrence Mann was going to re-start his writing career after experiencing what was actually going on in that cornfield… My movie was about fathers and sons, the love of baseball and how it transcends generations, about that complicated relationship between Ray and his father, and about forgiveness. That game of catch between Ray and his father…what a wonderful scene that turned out to be! These Hollywood people were good to Ann (Kinsella's wife) and me, we were on the set every day, saw them shoot every scene, they included us in discussions and decisions, and they took a *mediocre* book and turned it into a wonderful movie."

You could have heard a pin drop, cut the tension with a knife, or find your own cliché to describe a very awkward moment. I think we all wanted to hug Chris Messenger who never saw it coming.

When Kinsella finished his rant, the moderator nervously grabbed the microphone.

"Well, our next speakers are Mr. Sheinkopf and Professor Crepeau from the University of Central Florida." Dick came over to me and whispered in my ear: "we're screwed." Only he didn't say screwed. We were about to read Kinsella, in front of an already-annoyed Kinsella. And now we've seen what might be a typical response from an unpredictably eccentric man.

Here goes nothing …

We presented and discussed Kinsella's Eddie Scissons character.

I shared some of my favorite stories of my own brushes with The Syndrome, many of which I've covered in the previous chapters. Crepeau lent substance and credibility to our paper, and he called on audience members to "contemplate the complexity of the human mind and the fragility of the ego" when considering those who spin baseball half-truths and lies into cherished memories. He is a much more generous and kinder person than I am. I just call them liars.

After our presentation, Kinsella worked his way through the crowd and approached me with his business card in hand. He was reaching in my direction, wanting to write his new phone number on the back of his card before presenting it to me. I thought he was trying to shake my hand, so I grabbed his hand and shook it.

Dr. Richard C. Crepeau

Crepeau so lovingly pointed out, *"No, you idiot! He wants your pen, not your hand!"*

I got the handshake anyway and some memorable, very kind words from Kinsella. "That was wonderful! Please send me your book when it gets published," he told me. I wasn't writing a book then, but I did send him the paper when it was finally published in ARETE (the SLA Journal), a few months later. Well, 35 years later, here we are. And I so regret Bill Kinsella is no longer alive to finally get his copy of the book he inspired.

After dinner one evening at the conference, Kinsella and I played catch and he signed the ball for me: "*Go the distance, Bill Kinsella*" I still have that old beat up baseball, one of my favorites in a collection of Hall of Famers and favorite players on clean baseballs... It serves as a reminder that bringing a ball and glove with you wherever you go is always a good idea.

Dick and I engaged Kinsella in a lengthy discussion that evening after our lively game of catch. He told us that the Scissons character was based on a man he met in Iowa City, and the circumstances of their meeting were almost exactly as portrayed in the novel. Kinsella went on to tell us he had met a large number of Eddie Scissons Syndrome sufferers over the years, and that's why he was so entertained by our presentation.

It was reassuring to know we were not alone. And of course, since that time, I have been reassured of that many, many times.

It seems trite but necessary to thank the late author, but there is so much to thank him for. Kinsella coined the term "Eddie Scissons Syndrome," and without that character claiming to be the oldest living Chicago Cub, we would have to dream up a random term for this malady, and trust me, it would not be as good. In spite of not making the cut to become a movie star, Eddie's role in the book is so consequential, that it has spawned a new conversation, as relevant today as it was when it first came into being in the 1980s, and sadly, as it will be for future generations.

Unfortunately, this epidemic has not been eradicated, but thanks to Kinsella, we can all agree on what to call it.

Chapter 8

WAYNE MAHOOD'S GENTLE PRODDING

Beyond Dick Crepeau and Bill Kinsella, a few others have inspired me to keep this research going. One of the most prominent was Dr. Wayne Mahood, everyone's favorite professor from my college days, who became fascinated when I shared with him a copy of my first paper on this topic

It was a great privilege to have become Wayne's friend over the last forty years or so of his life, and we regularly stayed in touch from my graduation in 1973 until 2019 when he died after living a remarkable life and influencing thousands of students to go on and become teachers, or simply make an impact on society. His charge to us was to be kind, be curious and be productive. He was all three, for 85 years, and challenged his students to be the same. Wayne no doubt had similar conversations and scenarios with dozens if not hundreds of other former students with whom he stayed in touch. He always told me how fascinated he was with this Eddie Scissons topic, and I should try to "do something with it." In large part because of Wayne continually prodding me, I never put the project at the bottom of the pile and from time to time, I kept working at it.

Wayne and I corresponded about Eddie Scissons Syndrome off and on for many years, and this excerpt from his letter, dated July 25,1990, was especially worth saving:

"You know, an odd thing that is happening to me is that I am beginning to wonder about my own memory. That is, I know (there are records) that I played various college sports, but for the life of me, I'm not sure it ever happened. I even wonder whether I imagined doing some things. A funny experience occurred years ago when I met the president of a local insurance agency who said he played quarterback at the University of Rochester in the fall of my freshman year. That struck a bell with me for I thought we (Hamilton College) had played the University of Rochester that fall. Since I am a terrible pack rat, I was not surprised to find a starting line-up for the game and saw my name (which helped me realize I wasn't nuts), but his name did not appear. I still don't know what to think about it."

Dr. Wayne Mahood

It does make you wonder if insurance agencies breed the Eddie Scissons virus… or is this just a coincidence?

It's Not over until we say it's over

Over the years, this topic has developed a life of its own, and I've consistently given presentations for whoever will have me: Rotary, Kiwanis Clubs, SABR (the Society for American Baseball Research), NINE, SLA, you name it, I've done it.

I gave what I thought would be the final word on this topic in a paper at the Cooperstown Symposium on Baseball and American Culture at the Baseball Hall of Fame in June 2023—admittedly, a (the?) high point of my life.

At the Hall of Fame, I was the last presenter on the last day of the conference, and by the time I presented, a lot of people had already gone home—there were fewer than 100 people left in attendance. I compared myself to a relief pitcher at Dodger Stadium where most fans arrive late and leave early. I was doing mop-up duty in a blowout game where most fans have gone home to beat the rush.

"For those who stayed, thank you. Your presence here means a lot to me," I told them.

It couldn't have been a better audience, and it was magical to share my message with them. When it was over, many of them waited in line to tell me *their* stories—each one had a story that was more shocking than the one before.

We had the greatest time, listening to each other's ESS experiences. We finally had to move along as the clean-up crew was kicking us out. The program was over, and the staff wanted to go home. Indeed, it was like the end of a game, and the ushers were politely telling us to leave.

One of those who stayed after the presentation was another

highly respected college professor, writer of some pretty terrific baseball books, and valued friend, James Walker, who came up to me and suggested I write a book on this subject. It hadn't occurred to me there was still more to say on this matter until my wife and I returned to our home in Florida and I was able to revisit the file cabinet full of ESS *stuff* I had amassed over the years.

Jim's encouragement meant a lot to me. Jim and his wife, Judith Hiltner wrote the award winning biography on Red Barber, among other brilliantly written baseball books, and his opinion carried a lot of weight.

Maybe Jim was right. Maybe this topic had wider appeal than I'd realized. I suspect because so many people have been affected by this ESS virus, these stories are still relevant.

I had accumulated a lot of material related to Eddie Scissons Syndrome and thought it might be time to clean out that filing cabinet. The files contained personal notes and newspaper articles, postcards, letters, copies of emails and pictures. They contained cassette tapes with valuable interviews, a VHS tape but no place to watch it anymore, articles from local and national newspapers and magazines, and correspondence from friends, many of whom were no longer living.

I'm so glad I've held onto everything. All of that insightful research represents the backbone of this book.

Whenever I present to a group, one question typically gets asked the most frequently: "why?" Why would someone go through life trying to pass themselves off as a former major leaguer? Why would someone lie about it, knowing that embarrassment and humiliation was inevitable if they were found out. It was a question I often asked myself. And a few years ago, in preparation for a paper on this topic I was about to give, I interviewed a highly respected psychotherapist friend who offered his educated opinion on a matter where we all have opinions but no answers.

Chapter 9

WHY?

Why would someone lie about playing Major League Baseball?

It's a question I've wondered about many times during all these years exploring Eddie Scissons Syndrome.

I know there were many reasons, some obvious, some hidden, and not surprisingly when confronted, some were not very forthcoming with an answer. The chiropractor who attended fantasy camp told me it was "good for his business," but he obviously basked in the celebrity status this lie afforded him, with all the beautifully framed photos and posters of himself in a Yankee uniform. He had no shame in telling me that, knowing it was shameful lie! I suspect his claim that it was "good for business" might be truthful, but he also knew it was a smokescreen for living a fantasy and enjoying the perks of a celebrity status he hadn't earned.

Several years ago, as I prepared a presentation on this topic, I interviewed a psychologist friend and colleague at the University of Central Florida, Dr. Robert Harman, to help me better understand the motivation of men lying about playing major league baseball.

"We admire major league ballplayers, and someone who

claims that status has instant respect," Dr. Harman told me. "We see them as uniquely important celebrities with the set of athletic skills and talent we wish we had. We admire them. They are our heroes. But for the liar, there's a sense of living a fantasy, escaping from his humdrum everyday life and creating this alternate reality of being a professional athlete. The real danger here is when, in extreme cases, the person starts to believe his own lie."

"In some cases, liars try to compensate for feelings of inadequacy or lack of accomplishment in their own life. This might be their way of fulfilling their long held fantasy of being a professional baseball player, by lying and getting others to believe their lie. And by getting people to believe their lie, that they played professional baseball, their lives are suddenly more interesting, and they gain social acceptance."

Dr. Harman made a distinction about the types of lies someone tries to pass off and their reasoning. Yes, the chiropractor trying to gain trust and influence with his patients is dishonest.

"But more disgusting are those guys who misrepresent themselves, telling a woman they were a professional athlete to deceive them into becoming a romantic partner," he said. "You hear about cases like this where the guy takes advantage of the woman financially as well because he has established himself as this celebrity athlete, just in need of a temporary loan or her investment in a 'sure thing.' This kind of social manipulation, deception, and ultimately criminal behavior is reprehensible."

Dr. Harman also noted how Eddie Scissons Syndrome sufferers face risk by passing off lies about something that can be easily refuted. All it takes is someone cracking open the "Big Mac" or visiting Baseball Reference's website and checking a name or team roster.

"I'm intrigued by the liar who knows that exposure would bring humiliation, public embarrassment and damage to his reputation, and yet he willingly takes the risk," Dr. Harman said. "Yet he still takes a chance at getting caught, and losing the trust of friends, family, and colleagues."

Yes, there are risks. But there are certainly rewards. People look at you differently when they think you played in the big leagues. And I suspect that it can be a great feeling.

When considering the many reasons people have for lying, two specific motives—to obtain rewards, and to win the admiration of others—are commonly aligned with Eddie Scissons Syndrome. Some liars even experience a euphoric "duping delight" from passing off a lie.

Tim Keown, writing for ESPN, authored a story in 2013 about people who inflate their athletic accomplishments, such as one man who claimed (falsely) to have played for Ohio State's football team.

As Keown wrote, "My guess is he just wanted to be somebody. And he was, too, probably for far longer than even he expected."

The closest I ever came to getting a substantive reason for Eddie Scissons Syndrome came from a friend of mine, Dr. Julian J. Szucko, a retired psychotherapist who researched and wrote about the many facets of the use and misuse of lie detectors. Recognized as a leading expert in his field, Dr. Szucko had this answer for me when I posed the question of *why* to him. He threw his hands up in the air. "Y'know, it's probably just fun for them to lie," he said. Maybe it's just that simple.

Chapter 10

THE MOST INFAMOUS CASE OF ESS

Paul H. Dunn was one of the highest-ranking and most beloved figures in the Church of Jesus Christ of Latter-day Saints.

Dunn's vast popularity was based on an uncanny ability to tell gripping stories at Mormon conferences and from the pulpit, sermons and lectures in more than a dozen books, and on cassette tapes about his time as a professional baseball player with the St. Louis Cardinals, and about his heroism during a career as a combat veteran in World War II.

He claimed, as a boy in Arkansas, to have befriended Lou Gehrig when the Yankees came to Little Rock for an exhibition game. It was a story that Dunn told again and again—how the "Iron Horse" called on Dunn to pitch to him and offered the boy guidance that would transform his life.

He claimed, after being signed by the Cardinals, to have been farmed out to the Hollywood Stars of the Pacific Coast League and the Pocatello club in the Pioneer League.

He claimed to have been in spring training with Stan Musial

and pitched to Joe DiMaggio and Ted Williams.

He claimed to have spent four or five years playing professional baseball, including reaching the major leagues with the Cardinals.

He claimed that his baseball career ended because of an injury.

One of Dunn's favorite baseball stories involved his time playing in Pocatello. As Dunn recalled, he was pitching in the eighth inning of a playoff game with no score when the opposing team's batter hit a sharp single up the middle to the center fielder. It should have been an easy score for the runner on second, yet the ball was apparently hit so hard that he was thrown out in a close call at the plate.

As Dunn describes it, this player began to scream obscenities at the umpire, which got him ejected from the game. As Dunn returned to the mound, the ump supposedly told him, "Paul, forgive him, he doesn't understand." (Perhaps reminiscent of Jesus's words, "Forgive them, Father, for they do not know what they do.")

Dunn told another of his favorite baseball tales at the church's General Conference in 1980. Dunn explained at the end of the talk how willing he was to share his faith with his fellow teammates. The story begins with his manager knocking on Dunn's hotel room door:

> "He said, 'Paul, may I come in?'
>
> And I said, 'Please do. What's the matter?'
>
> He said, 'Close the door, and whatever you do don't tell the others I came.'
>
> I said, 'Well, I won't.'
>
> He responded: 'I've been watching you for these past two months. You know the Lord, don't you?'

I said, 'I think he's my friend.'

He said, 'Would you help me find him?'

We sat down in the room, and for over two hours talked about God, the Eternal Father, and his Son, Jesus Christ. Tears began to form in his eyes.

I said, 'Danny, have you ever prayed?'

He said, 'No.'

I said, 'Would it offend you to pray with me?'

'Well,' he said, 'not if you will pray.'

I said, 'I would be honored.'

So together we knelt down beside my bed and talked to Heavenly Father. We took time-out. And as we arose from our knees, he pushed back the tears, threw his arms around me, almost choked me to death, and said, 'Thank you, thank you. Could we do this some more?'

I said, 'As often as you would like.'

We did on several other occasions. But you know what was interesting. Before the season ended, several other knocks came at my door. One night it was the first baseman, then the shortstop, and the left fielder. And each in his own wonderful way said, 'Don't tell the others.'"[3]

The problem? Dunn fabricated all of it.

He never met Lou Gehrig.

He was never signed by the Cardinals.

He never played for the Hollywood Stars or the Pocatello Cardinals.

---

[3] https://www.churchofjesuschrist.org/study/general-conference/1980/04/time-out?lang=eng

He never reached the majors, never played with or met Stan Musial in spring training, and never pitched to Ted Williams and Joe DiMaggio.

In fact, his entire professional baseball career amounted to one game with the Ontario Orioles in the "Class C" Sunset League in 1947. After pitching with Ontario in exhibition action, he came on in relief during the team's opening regular season game against Riverside. By the end of the week, he was released, and he would never play again.

These were not *embellishments*, they were outright lies. Dunn's stories were not based upon any facts, just fabricated stories told over and over to make himself into a super-hero to his devoted followers. We don't know if he actually started to believe his own lies, some people do. But for decades, his lies went completely unchecked by the church, allowing him to acquire ill-gotten money, status and admiration.

Unlike many ESS sufferers whose stories are rather harmless, Dunn's lies had real consequences.

In the late 1970s and early 1980s, Dunn relied on goodwill largely built on his war and baseball stories in promoting an investment scheme, AFCO Enterprises, that caused tremendous pain and financial ruin to hundreds of followers. Having Dunn's name attached to the company made people more trusting of it. But AFCO was a classic Ponzi scheme—and many investors lost their life savings, their homes or the tens of thousands of dollars they invested.[4]

Dunn's lies about his baseball career unraveled, in large part, because of the AFCO coverup—and because finally someone was willing to stand up to Dunn and to the church that had protected

[4] Packer, Lynn Kenneth. *Lying for the Lord: The Paul H. Dunn Stories.* CreateSpace Independent Publishing Platform, 2015.

him and his lies for decades.

That person was investigative journalist Lynn Packer, who was threatened with the loss of his job as BYU journalism professor if he reported what he'd uncovered (at the time, Packer's wife was battling cancer). In the face of Packer's research, the church decided to shift Dunn to Emeritus status—and the journalist's teaching contract wasn't renewed, in part, because it was a violation of church and university policies to publicly criticize church leaders.

Packer's reporting was purchased by *The Arizona Republic* and finally brought to light in 1991.

Even then, Dunn couldn't admit that he lied. He simply *combined* stories. He claimed that audiences could better connect to his stories about the Cardinals than his actual meager baseball career. He couldn't just come clean and admit to lying about his baseball and military careers.

"The combining of stories seems justifiable in terms of illustrating a point. My motives are pure and innocent," he told the Republic in 1991. "I haven't purposely tried to embellish or rewrite history. I've tried to illustrate points that would create interest."[5]

To be clear, Dunn did not embellish anything, didn't exaggerate or overstate. He fabricated these stories, made up everything, based upon nothing. What he did was shamefully lie, and then lied some more in a half-assed attempt to clarify his position. And he never admitted to nor apologized for lying.

But the church later issued a statement on Dunn's behalf: "I confess that I have not always been accurate in my public talks and writings." As Packer noted later, the words lie, fake, or fabricate hadn't been used—but a partial admission was better than no admission.

---

[5] Robertson, Richard R. "Mormon Leader Admits Exaggerating Stories." *The Arizona Republic*, 16 Feb. 1991, p. B10.

In his book, *Lying for the Lord: The Paul H. Dunn Stories*, Packer details the lies Dunn told and repeated over the years, the attempted coverup by church elders, and the reactions from Dunn's followers.

Among the most damning facts? A writer for the church's magazine, *New Era,* found out Dunn's baseball stories were false *in 1970,* only for nothing to happen. No confrontation, no articles or tell-all pieces in Life Magazine, no buzz around a possible scandal in the church… but seven years later, a similar situation happened, as Packer recounted in his book:

Norman Olsen—the president of the Mormon mission in St. Louis "invited Dunn to bring Donny and Marie Osmond to St. Louis for a Mormon Night at a (St. Louis) Cardinals baseball game at Busch Stadium. Because Dunn had played for the Cardinals, Olsen thought it would be a nice surprise to present Dunn with a plaque inscribed with the years he played, in front of thousands of fans. So, Olsen had missionaries go to the Cardinals' vast baseball library to get that information. To the missionaries' amazement, the librarian could not find a trace of Dunn pitching for the major league team or for any of its multiple farm clubs. The plaque idea was quietly dropped, but the word got out."[6] This time, in 1977, "the word got out" as Packer stated in his book. So, what changed?

The saga of Paul Dunn is one of the most infamous and tragic cases of the Syndrome I have encountered, and I encourage future ESS researchers to invest the time and energy to uncover the many layers of lies and cult worship that provided the backdrop to this fascinating, but in the end, very sad case.

---

[6] Packer, Lynn Kenneth. *Lying for the Lord: The Paul H. Dunn Stories*. CreateSpace Independent Publishing Platform, 2015.

Chapter 11

PATTERNS

If you pay close enough attention, you might be able to find those guys who have contracted the ESS virus among your circle of friends, co-workers, even your extended family. The imposters seem to gravitate toward specific backgrounds or careers.

Or they might try to pass off their baseball glory in job applications.

Let's explore some of the most common patterns and trends of Baseball Imposters.

Pattern #1: Vague stories

If you talk to true big leaguers, they *remember* pitch sequences and important at-bats. They recall that 3-2 slider they threw in the dirt to strike out the all-star first baseman. They remember so vividly because those moments reflect their glory days. ESS sufferers often have trouble remembering specific details ... because those details *didn't* happen, and because they may not have ever been challenged to really remember them.

Where have you gone, Bobby Movallo?

During the late 1990s, I brought a few members of the admissions staff with me to an office furniture store in Atlanta where we were looking to furnish our newly renovated admissions office space. It was a simple task, sit behind some desks and try out some desk chairs… decide which ones suited our needs and help me put together a proposal. How could conversation with the sales associate possibly become controversial, and why would baseball even become part of the story? I don't know how, but it did. I guess with me, all roads lead to baseball, and this venture was no exception.

Bobby Movallo looked like he could have been an athlete a few years before, so when he told us that he played for the Oakland A's in 1989, it seemed credible. They had a great year in '89, so I had a few questions, and his answers did not disappoint. As the story unfolded, he told us he played centerfield but came to bat only once in the Big Leagues. And that at-bat happened in game two of the 1989 World Series. Surprisingly, he could remember no other details from that game: when (in what inning) he came to bat and under what circumstances. Who was pitching? He couldn't remember. And *he thinks* he flied out to center field. He *thinks*! My jaw dropped. Only my colleagues' compassion for this obvious liar prevented me from drilling down. They had seen me in action before and knew where this was going, so their compassion for Bobby made them step in before things got ugly. I understand why they put the brakes on my interrogation, but there was so much I wanted to know, so many questions to be asked, so many lies to be told. I still have his business card, with notes on the back from our conversation. I sometimes wonder what might have come from following up.

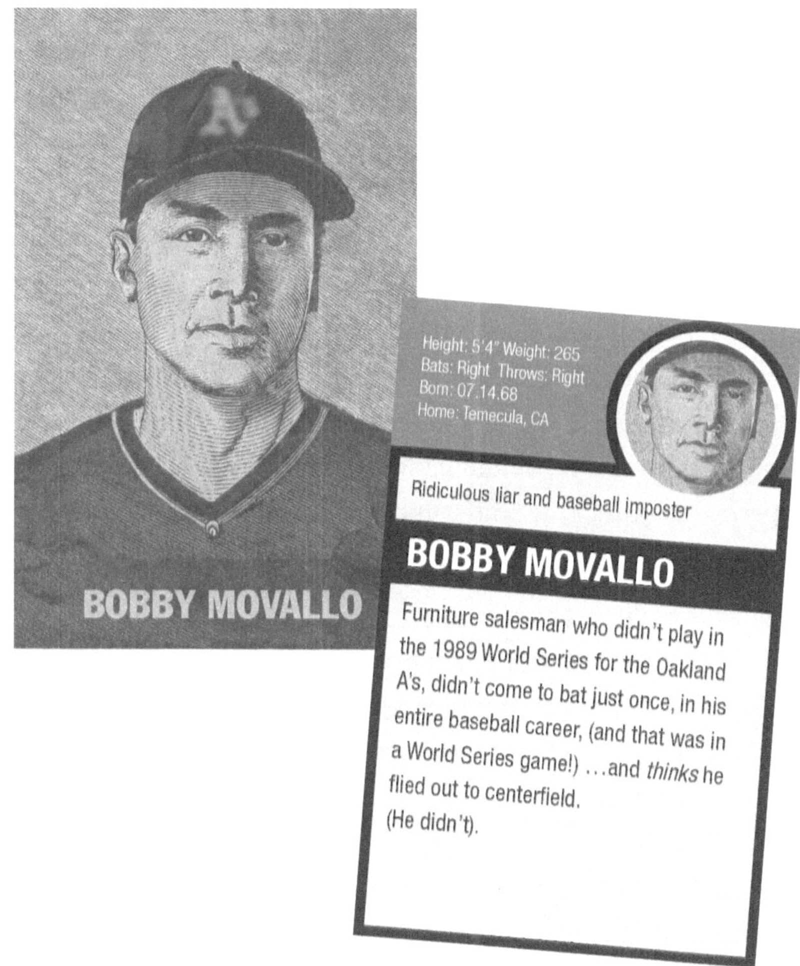
BOBBY MOVALLO

Height: 5'4" Weight: 265
Bats: Right Throws: Right
Born: 07.14.68
Home: Temecula, CA

Ridiculous liar and baseball imposter

BOBBY MOVALLO

Furniture salesman who didn't play in
the 1989 World Series for the Oakland
A's, didn't come to bat just once, in his
entire baseball career, (and that was in
a World Series game!) ...and *thinks* he
flied out to centerfield.
(He didn't).

Lying is not very neighborly

I really enjoyed getting to know "Big Al." As neighbors, we became friends over many months, and I valued his friendship.

Living in Davenport, Iowa for a brief time, our neighbor, Allen Turner, told me of his experiences playing for the Pittsburgh Pirates in the 1950s and early '60s.

Allen was in his fifties, and his former athletic build from decades prior had given way to a beer gut. He was still bitter about the way black players like himself were treated throughout the South and elsewhere. He recalled that he wasn't allowed to stay in the same hotels with his teammates and was frequently denied a table at restaurants where his teammates ate. He was bitter, and given his experiences, he had every right to be. He would get me riled up with these conversations, injustices we have all heard about and reacted to, but now I was talking to a guy who actually experienced Jim Crow South first-hand. And it made me angry.

But when the conversation turned to actual baseball of the 1960's, not just the cultural history of the time, I thought it was odd that he couldn't remember the names of most of his teammates, and the ones he did remember seemed to be the ones everyone had heard of. Turner couldn't remember Danny Murtaugh being his manager but was "very close friends with Roberto Clemente and Willie Stargell." His baseball stories were hazy and nonspecific. I chalked that up to his being in his 50's, a very old man by my standards at that time, and I had heard that people sometimes had problems with memory as they grew old. But as a former big leaguer, Allen had my respect. It didn't dawn on me to check his story until I had my very own copy of the Big Mac many years later and I found out the shocking truth.

I couldn't believe my eyes when I discovered *The Baseball Encyclopedia* failed to include "Big Al" (as he said he was called by "Clemente and some of the other guys") in their thorough listing of every major league baseball player since 1876. I had even given my friend Allen my hardcover edition of Roberto Clemente's biography, thinking he was probably mentioned in it (he wasn't).

Allen didn't seem like the kind of guy who made stuff up just to impress a neighbor, but sadly, I guess he was.

We're warning you, Lorenzo...

From my friend, Jay Thomas, author, professor, entrepreneur, and former visiting team batboy for the Chicago Cubs:

In April 2017, my daughter Claire and I decided to catch a rainy afternoon Washington Nationals game, and because of the lousy weather, we were able to grab some cheap tickets for one of the luxury suites behind home plate.

The hostess mentioned that one of the regulars in the suite was a fellow who had played in the Negro Leagues. He was well into his nineties and was something of a legend among Nationals fans, who were used to seeing him at every home game. In fact, he was later celebrated on the field by the Nationals before a World Series game.

Lorenzo showed up in the second inning and invited us to sit with him and talk baseball.

He told us he had played for the Baltimore Elite Giants (pronounced "ee-light" by players of the day) and was a shortstop, as I recall. Our conversation was at first about playing baseball, bus trips, fans and life in the Negro Leagues.

I asked him which players he had played against and with. Not surprisingly, he mentioned Satchel Paige and Larry Doby and Josh Gibson—players who most fans could name. I told him that I knew quite a bit about players from his era and gave him a few names. But his memory began getting a bit hazy. So, I changed the subject to places and ballparks that he might have played in. Negro League teams often shared stadiums with big league teams like Wrigley Field and Comiskey Park, and minor league ballparks as well. He could not name a single stadium, which struck me as odd, but then his answers became suspiciously vague.

"I didn't really pay attention to where we were playing," he told me. "I was just playing because I loved the game."

When I returned back home to Chicago, I tracked down an encyclopedia of Negro League teams and players. He was not listed as having played for any team.

Still, I held out hope, so I reached out to the Negro Leagues Baseball Museum. I received a prompt response assuring me that, no, our friend in Washington had never played for the Baltimore Elite Giants—or any other Negro League team.

Sounds like ESS has yet claimed another poor soul.

Thanks, Jay. I too was unable to find any information that would support Lorenzo's story. But I might chalk up Lorenzo's age ("he was well into his nineties") to a somewhat faulty memory, and the less than reliable records kept by the Negro Leagues from that era that keep us from knowing for certain if his story actually checks out. So, we are not quite ready to welcome Lorenzo into the ESS Club. We'll give him a pass, for now.

But if we find a shred of evidence, just a shred, Lorenzo, you may be inducted into the Eddie Scissons Syndrome (*not so exclusive*) Club at some point in the future. Be forewarned.

Pattern #2: Applications for jobs, college admission, and who knows what else?

Job applications present a perfect opportunity to uncover Baseball Imposters.

Lots of people lie on their resumes. In fact, one 2023 job applicant behavior survey found that 70% of workers confessed to lying on their resumes—and 37% admit to lying frequently.[7]

People lie about all sorts of things on their resumes, from embellishing responsibilities and how many people they manage all the way to making up entire positions and fabricating their awards or accolades.

Fabricating a big league career out of thin air also can help to cover up those pesky career gaps. If you were slugging away in the minors and majors, no wonder you weren't working in a typical job.

That was the case when my brother called me one day many years ago, excited that he had interviewed a former major league baseball player for a job at the Florida Solar Energy Center where he worked. He read me the resume of Chuck Schaad, telling of his experience pitching for the San Francisco Giants. As if that wasn't enough, Schaad also claimed he had played in the NFL for the New Orleans Saints. Unfortunately, Chuck's name was omitted from the Big Mac, and while I never checked, I suspect his name would also not be found in any similar publication for those who played in the NFL. Apparently, these guys think people won't check up on stuff like that.

By the way, maybe his ridiculous lies had nothing to do with it, but Chuck Schaad was not offered the job at the Florida Solar Energy Center.

---

[7] "Should You Lie on Your Resume? The Risks of Lying to Get a Job." *ResumeLab*, 2023, www.resumelab.com/career-advice/lying-to-get-a-job.

Similarly, in my role as Admissions Director at three different universities, I collected seventeen (seventeen!) copies of admissions applications showing responses about past work experience including the following: "St. Louis Cardinals," "New York Yankees," "Atlanta Braves," "San Francisco Giants," and "Pittsburgh Pirates." None of them had the word "organization" after the big league team's name. Checking the Big Mac and Baseball-Reference.com, I was disappointed but not surprised to see none of the applicants actually played major league baseball. None! Some had *brief* minor league experience, none higher than Class A, verified on Baseball-Reference.com, but most had nothing.

I suppose as Admissions Director, I could have (maybe *should have*) taken action to expose their misstatement. Lying on an admissions application is no small thing, but the reality was these were not stellar students in the first place, they weren't applying for medical school admission, and it was apparent from their dismal transcripts and test score reports that they would not be competitive. Since none of them were actually admitted anyway, why fight that battle? Let them peddle their lies somewhere else.

Pattern #3: Unsuspecting relatives

It's common for someone's lies to go undetected by their unsuspecting family such as later-in-life wives and stepchildren. They're so *proud* to learn their stepfather played pro baseball… the kind of lie that comes back to haunt them when families compile information to be used in an obituary.

Maybe he should have fact-checked his dad

Hunter Dobbins was pitching in his first Major League season in 2025 when he found himself in the middle of a major rivalry—and connected to a classic case of modern-day Eddie Scissons Syndrome.

The Red Sox rookie, ahead of his team facing the Yankees, claimed in an interview that he'd rather walk away from baseball than play for the Yankees.

"If the Yankees were the last team to give me a contract, I'd retire," he said.[8]

Dobbins claimed that his animosity stemmed, in part, from the way the Yankees had treated his father, former pitcher Lance Dobbins.

"He was actually drafted twice by the Yankees," Hunter told the Boston Herald. "Signed with them his last year and then he got traded over to the Diamondbacks."

Except he didn't. Those claims were revealed to be false, with no record of Lance ever being drafted by the Yankees even once, or ever playing for them.

Also false? Lance Dobbins' claims to being "good friends" with former Yankees hurler Andy Pettitte. In fact, Pettitte stated he had no recollection of Lance Dobbins.

The son later clarified that he'd simply repeated the stories he'd heard growing up.

"At the end of the day, it's just from my dad and what I kind of grew my love for the game. At the end of the day, I don't go fact-check my dad or anything like that."[9]

Lance Dobbins, like many ESS sufferers, played some organized

---

[8] Starr, Gabrielle. "Red Sox-Yankees: Hunter Dobbins Rivalry, MLB Fans, Andy Pettitte, New York vs. Boston." *Boston Herald*, 7 June 2025, www.bostonherald.com/2025/06/07/red-sox-yankees-hunter-dobbins-rivalry-mlb-baseball-fans-andy-pettitte-new-york-boston/.

[9] Schwartz, Jared. "Red Sox's Hunter Dobbins Blames Dad for False Yankees Claims." *New York Post*, 11 June 2025, nypost.com/2025/06/11/sports/red-soxs-hunter-dobbins-blames-dad-for-false-yankees-claims/.

baseball—two seasons of independent league baseball in 1996 and 1997. But that's it.

Sadly, cases of Eddie Scissons Syndrome often affect children and other relatives. They grow up hearing these grandiose stories and, when they start to investigate, they wind up hitting unexpected walls.

Bring in the left-hander

Upon entering the service department at my local Volvo dealer in Las Vegas, I couldn't believe my eyes …I saw my name on the white board, just below that of "Jerry Reuss." We both had 8:30 a.m. appointments to get our Volvos serviced.

How could it be possible that the great Dodgers pitcher was also getting his car serviced at the Volvo dealer on Sahara at the same time as me? Might that be a common name, and some guy also named Jerry Reuss with a Volvo that needed servicing, was hanging around the waiting room while his car was getting its oil changed?

Is this the same Jerry Reuss who played in the big leagues for more than two decades, who pitched a no-hitter, was an All-Star, and won a World Series title?

Does *The* Jerry Reuss drive a Volvo, like me?

As I entered the waiting area in the service department, there he was. It was unmistakable. The real Jerry Reuss, not just a guy with the same name. The real Jerry Reuss was the only customer waiting for his car. And he was waiting like any other civilian. He was Jerry Reuss, for chrissakes! He shouldn't be in a waiting room with a guy like me, eager to pepper him with questions about his baseball career (and about his Volvo). But this was Jerry Reuss, and he couldn't have been nicer and more engaging in our conversation, acting like he wasn't annoyed, but I suspect he was. How could he not be annoyed? I can be pretty annoying, and couple that with a chance to talk with a baseball legend, who also drives a Volvo, and you've got a deadly combination.

Afterward, I went out and bought his book on Amazon, (where, by the way, you can also buy this book!). I read it cover to cover, and despite his affiliation with the Dodgers, I became a Jerry Reuss fan. Since we both live in Las Vegas and both drive Volvos, I figured I might see him around and we could talk baseball, or Volvos. Of course that didn't happen.

What ended up happening was almost better than that. I got a great ESS story out of it.

At my next visit to the Volvo dealer for regular maintenance, I found myself in the waiting room by myself until a tall, very attractive, nicely dressed and athletically built woman in her mid to late forties entered. She immediately struck up a conversation about the baseball book I was reading. I told her I met Jerry Reuss the last time I was there, and she quickly responded with a comment that they were good friends with the Reusses because her husband was Jerry's teammate with the Cubs (one of the few teams Jerry never played for during his 22-year career!). I didn't know that then, or it may have raised a very large red flag… or I might have challenged her with that fact.

It seems, her husband (told her) he had played for the Cubs, Cardinals and Reds before they met. She was much younger than her husband and her interest in athletics was limited to being a college swimmer at Northern Illinois. She told me she knew very little about baseball before meeting her husband who had retired from professional baseball before they even met. She said several times how much I would enjoy knowing her hedge fund manager husband, with his love for the game beyond his playing days.

I asked her husband's name, can't remember it now, but it was a fairly WASPish, common name… vaguely familiar as those kinds of names tend to be, and that he was possibly one of those who was telling the truth. I was to find out that common names are always vaguely familiar, and that upon looking him up in every possible source, I found he never played professional baseball, at any level. He had carried that lie with him throughout his adulthood and had been lying to his wife since they met some 11 years before. When I finally did meet him at a fundraiser for UNLV athletics, his wife told him that I was the one she had told him about. We had a brief, superficial conversation, after which I told him to please pass along my regards to his former teammate Jerry Reuss, before he nervously shuffled off with his unsuspecting wife to the silent auction.

I don't remember this guy's name, but believe me, I checked every source available. He never played anywhere. Baseball Reference.com doesn't get it wrong. I can't lie to my wife about anything because I know she'd know I was lying, like about already having had a cookie earlier in the day while she was working or just looking the other way.

But about big stuff like having played for three major league teams before we met?

How does this guy get away with that? I need to know his secret.

And another question I keep asking… "What is wrong with people?"

There's no "Pretender's List," but if there were…

In a letter to me after some opportunity to discuss the Syndrome, Paul A., an executive at Hewlett-Packard, wrote:

I heard your talk on the Eddie Scissons thing, and it got me thinking. Not long ago, I was contacted by a young lady here at work, whose fiancé's father claimed to have played for the Brooklyn Dodgers. I looked him up, John Wernette II is nowhere to be found in any of the references. I even contacted the Sporting News archives and there was no record of him playing minor league ball either. Has he ever turned up on your pretenders list?

Paul, There is no "pretenders list." But it's a nice idea, and if there were such a list, John Wernette II would be on it. By the way, that list would be pretty long, and John would be in good company with many fine people who just don't think they'll get caught. Wernette's name is not in The Big Mac or anywhere else that reliable records are kept on this important matter.

A 'good' story… (*couldn't resist*)

Dan Good, a book ghostwriter and the author of *Playing Through the Pain,* a biography of All-Star third baseman Ken Caminiti, shared a story about a man discussing his father's so-called pro baseball career.

Quite a few years ago, I was collaborating with a public figure and humanitarian who, knowing my interest in baseball, mentioned his personal connection to the game.

"Before I was born in the 1930s, my father enjoyed success playing in the minor leagues in the Pacific Coast League," he told me.

How exciting! That league featured lots of Major League talent—from stars like the DiMaggio brothers to journeymen such as outfielder Nino Bongiovanni. I took to Baseball-Reference.com and Newspapers.com looking for more information about this man's father and his days slumming around the PCL. I couldn't find anything. I searched for hours. Maybe the name was spelled differently, I thought, so I checked every possible rendition of Bongiovanni. Nothing worked.

I studied league rosters. Bupkis. I also found lots of newspaper mentions of the father, but not a single one had anything to do with baseball. For a lot of that time, he wasn't even living west of the Mississippi. It was disappointing to learn that the story wasn't true. I don't believe that my contact had any idea that his father lied about playing pro baseball, and I never brought it up with him, as I didn't want to puncture the myth. But the story stuck with me because of how confident and proud he was of his father, the imaginary baseball star. I'm quite sure he would have loved and admired his father regardless of his fake baseball career.

It turns out, Nino Bongiovanni played for the Cincinnati Redlegs in 1938 and 1939, coming to bat 166 times, hitting 43 singles and 7 doubles, driving in 17 runs. He was the 8467th player in MLB history. ESS researchers like us are grateful to BaseballReference.com for the resource to find the truth.

Nino Bongiovanni, 8467th player in MBL history

When researching cases of Eddie Scissons Syndrome, it's important to be thorough, to know where to look, and to not jump to conclusions.

Pattern #4: Cab drivers are especially susceptible to ESS

There is something about cab drivers, Uber drivers, and airport car rental shuttle drivers that makes them particularly susceptible to the Syndrome.

Cabbies will probably never see you again, they won't be held accountable, and there are seemingly no repercussions to lying. It might give the cabbie a sense of accomplishment and might even result in a bigger tip at the end of the ride. Plus, they get to live out this fantasy if only for a few minutes and feel what it's like to be thought of as a former Big Leaguer, as a celebrity. And there's no worry about getting found out, they'll never see you again, so who cares if you look it up?

I had a situation like that of my own in 1990 when I was heading to LaGuardia after a long, hot day in New York. The cab driver asked me where I was headed. I told him "Orlando," he responded with curiosity.

"I used to spend my spring trainings there when I was with the White Sox." Hmmm. The White Sox were typically associated with Tampa or Sarasota for their Florida Spring Training sites … and I thought only the Twins had ever called Orlando their Spring Training home.

"Were you in the White Sox *organization*?" I asked.

"No, I played in the majors with the White Sox, played with guys like Minnie Minoso and Billy Pierce. Ever hear of them?" I'm pretty sure he was annoyed with me for jumping to the *minor league* assumption, but c'mon. That was giving this guy a huge benefit of the doubt. Yea, I heard of them, but I so wanted to respond with "Sure of course I heard of them but I never heard of you … you must have collected baseball cards and had an active imagination." That's what I wanted to say but didn't. I also wanted to reach my destination, and not get my name in the paper the next morning.

I scratched down Mehrdad Medizahved's name and taxi license number displayed facing the passenger seat, just in case. I asked if he played under a different name, and he said, "No man, that's what made me so popular with the fans on the south side. They loved that I was a foreigner. It actually worked in my favor, you know, with the fans. I had quite a following." Yeah, sure, I thought …there were a lot of guys with similar names like that in the Big Leagues back then. Mehhrdad Mantle from Spavinaw, Oklahoma, of course, being one of the most popular, but he chose to be called Mickey… just because.

My friend Dick Crepeau had a similar experience when he and his wife, Pat, were leaving the Calgary Airport. They were the only passengers on the Alamo Shuttle headed to pick up their rental car.

When the driver asked, "Where are you from?" and Dick replied, with ensuing conversation that he worked at the University of Central Florida as a history professor , the driver responded, "That brings back memories of Spring Training when I was with the St. Louis Cardinals." The driver went on to say he played with some great Cardinal teams and players, like Bill White. He claimed he filled in for him at first base while White was injured.

"It was mostly a cup of coffee. Most of my career was in the minors."

That kind of humility adds a lot of credibility to the story, so much better than claiming he was an all-star or had won the Cy Young Award during his memorable Big League career.

Dick gave me his name when he got back to Orlando, and of course his story did not check out. The guy's name was Johnny Self, and I checked every spelling possible. There were guys with similar names, but they were born more than a hundred years ago, so it probably wasn't any of them. Ah well…

Now that we've covered some of the key patterns to look for, let's explore some of the files in a treasure trove of historical research being held in a tiny, baseball-obsessed town in upstate New York. Well, actually held in a Cloud these days… hovering over that charming village called Cooperstown.

Chapter 12
THE HOF IMPOSTERS FILE

The National Baseball Hall of Fame and Museum has been an incredible resource over the years in helping me acquire stories and research about Baseball Imposters.

After I started researching this topic, I visited their research wing—it's now named for Bart Giamatti, the former commissioner. I asked Librarian Cassidy Lent in advance of my visit, "Do you have any files about people who lie about being baseball players?"

Her response was quick, thorough and overwhelming.

Some of the saddest examples of Eddie Scissons Syndrome involve obituary details shared with the Hall of Fame asking for confirmation of the facts, or just more information about a former player's career. Unfortunately, the inquiry often necessitates the inevitable follow-up letter from the Hall of Fame informing the grieving family that your father, grandfather, or uncle never played major league baseball, and therefore the obituary contains information we cannot confirm.

The cases in the Hall of Fame files run the gamut from near-misses and half-truths to outright lies.

Responding to inquiries from the family is no easy task, but the Hall of Fame staff has had a lot of practice over the years and do so thoughtfully and respectfully:

"Unless your father was playing and managing under another name…"

So many letters from the Baseball Hall of Fame have this phrase embedded in their response to an inquiry from a loved one left behind seeking information about a career that never was. While playing under an assumed name may happen, it's a rare case, certainly not a common occurrence, but this helps them find another way to respectfully tell a family member their loved one is likely a liar.

"In our experience, about one out of five men who are said to have played major league or minor league baseball did not do so."

Pretty powerful statement from the Hall of Fame, based upon many years of experience with hundreds of cases and inquiries from survivors. I suppose this statement, in some small way, at least helps the survivor in knowing they are not alone.

And finally,

"I do not intend disrespect to your late [father, grandfather, uncle, etc.] However, before you invest more time and money in research, I thought you should know that _______'s baseball career (at least as stated in his obituary) did not take place."

That was the case for William Melvin Jr., an 82-year-old retired businessman whose obituary clearly states that he "pitched for the Philadelphia Phillies for a short time after college." Of course, there is no entry for him in any of the references that would confirm he indeed played in the Big Leagues. His family was dismayed to learn the truth after receiving one of the personalized, but standard letters from guys like Tim Wiles, retired research librarian at the Hall of Fame. This was a pretty common occurrence for him and his colleagues.

That also happened with the daughter of Al Boregart, who sent a letter to the Baseball Hall of Fame questioning if the photo she has of "the 1913 World Champion Philadelphia Athletics includes her father because he played for the A's until 1924 when he had to leave the team due to bad feet."

The response from the Hall of Fame revealed research that he may possibly be the same Al Boregart who signed a contract with the Class-D Cambridge (Maryland) Canners team in 1925, who was released later that year, but there is no record of an Al Boregart playing major league baseball. So, no, sorry…he's probably not

World Champion 1913 Philadelphia A's -- minus Al Boregart

in that team picture of the 1913 World Champs.

Namedropping: He played with Honus

Sometimes, name-dropping seems to add credence to a story by an Eddie Scissons Syndrome sufferer, of course, until fact-checking comes into play. The October 30, 1928, obituary for Peter Lavelle claims he "began his baseball career with the Holy Ghost

College nine. He later played sandlot ball with Honus Wagner and finally became a member of the Cincinnati club." I'm assuming they mean the Redlegs. It doesn't really matter because it seems his sandlot experience with Honus Wagner was the high point of his baseball career. So why throw in becoming "a member of the Cincinnati club"?

Records show that Lavelle did play for an Inter-State League (independent) team in 1895 that started in Steubenville, Ohio before moving to Akron and Lima—a team that a young John Peter Wagner also played for. So, his teaming with the Flying Dutchman does check out. I wonder if Honus, on his way to baseball immortality, bragged about having played with Lavelle back in Ohio at the start of his career.

The wrong Gleason

An obituary for Raymond F. Gleason in November 1974 stated he was 80 years old, retired chief clerk of the Chicago Board of Election Commissioners, having worked for the Board for fifty-seven years. It also stated he was a pitcher for the Chicago White Sox in 1911 and 1912. Notably, a White Sox coach in 1912, and later the team's manager, was "Kid" Gleason.

It makes me wonder…how many employees at the Chicago Board of Election Commissioners over the years heard exciting tales of Ray playing for the White Sox way back then? He didn't, according to every source available, or for their minor league affiliates (Baseball-Reference.com has no record of him playing minor league baseball either).

I'll bet his colleagues enjoyed hearing about his non-existent baseball career all those years. "Hey, there goes Ray, that guy who played for the White Sox! He's got such great stories about his playing days, what a guy! I think they called him "Kid."

Never a Senator

Meanwhile, an obit dated Oct. 15, 1974: "Thomas W. Gilligan, at sixty-seven, Ex-Major League Player… former star Harvard athlete and Big League baseball player, died… after a long illness." A graduate of Phillips-Exeter Academy, Harvard University, and Boston College Law School… That would be enough accomplishments for any one person in a lifetime, wouldn't you think? Elite boarding school, the best of the Ivy Leagues, law degree, probably a successful practice and fulfilling legal career … but somehow, that wasn't enough. It was important for someone to include in his obituary "and after graduation, he signed with the Washington Senators, playing with the team until an arm injury forced his retirement."

A 1931 Boston Globe article noted that Gilligan "recently went to Biloxi, Miss., with the Washington Senators." But, despite getting a look, Gilligan never played regular season baseball in the majors or minors. So, I guess he had to rely on his impressive resume minus a big league career with the Senators, to get by.

Short and sweet

The obit appeared in newspapers in 1927.

ALTON, Ill., June 27 (AP).—Jerry Dooley, who played baseball with the old St. Louis Browns under Charles Comisky, died here today. He was 82 years old.

Nice obit…short and sweet. Except Jerry never played professional baseball. Not for the St. Louis Browns, or anyone else!

This guy was some athlete!

An obit from November 1986 from St. Louis, Missouri celebrated the life of noted athlete Karl W. Hodge, 95.

Hodge's obit stated that he won the National Clay Courts senior singles in 1947 and 1948, and the senior indoor title in 1951. It also claimed that he was a pitcher for the old New York Giants before he entered the Army during World War I.

Not exactly. Newspaper records from 1913 and 1914 show that Hodge *tried out* with the St. Louis Browns, and later, the Giants. As one article noted, "The Giants brought with them from Chicago, Karl Hodge, a young pitcher. Hodge has not been signed but is to have a trial. He is a Williams College product and looks boyish for big league timber."[10] He traveled with the Giants and was on the team's payroll for a little while in 1914 but was later released.

Look, the guy accomplished a lot in his life. But somehow traveling with the Giants morphed into playing with the Giants. But he apparently was one heck of a tennis player!

A toothy excuse

James W. Lindley died April 20, 1990, as stated in the obit, "one of New Bedford's oldest residents." He was 105, so I imagine he indeed would be among New Bedford's oldest. To his credit, he never claimed to have actually played in the Big Leagues, just the old New England League, for Fall River and New Bedford." But "among his teammates, was Walter J. 'Rabbit' Maranville who went on to play with the Boston Braves." An obituary went on to state "Mr. Lindley was sold to the Boston Red Sox but quit playing after his teeth were knocked out by a ball."

Couldn't he just get dentures? Was that a good enough reason

10 The Republican 7/17/14

to give up the dream? And do you really need teeth to play baseball?

"Silver Bill"

William Stickney died December 17, 1932. His obit in the *Brooklyn Eagle* spoke to his long minor league baseball career, which accurately noted that he "moved to the Pacific Coast and played with San Francisco, Oakland and many other cities pioneering in baseball." All fine and supported by newspaper accounts.

Limited minor league stats show "Silver Bill" Stickney played fifty-six games over six seasons from 1886 to 1892. He batted .280 in 214 at bats, stole ten bases, and even hit one home run. He wore the uniform of the Acid Iron Earths of the Gulf League, for Mobile, the Little Rock Giants of the Southwest League, the Jackson Jaxons in the Tri-State league. He played for Stockton, the Oakland Colonels and finished his career with the Montgomery Lambs of the Southern Association in 1892. These were great minor league team names!

But there was an interesting addition to the obit: "After that came 'big league' play with Chicago and Cincinnati." *Hmm.*

There isn't any record of "Silver Bill" making it to the majors.

Wasn't his minor league experience enough? It's unclear who tried to puff up his baseball bonafides. It may have been Will himself who told the tale. It may have been the obit writer, or anyone in between. And just throwing that in at the end of the obit, burying the lead like that, was it really necessary?

This hit-and-run victim is …out!

On November 5, 1932, the *Brooklyn Eagle* posted an obituary with the headline, "*McVey, Old Oriole Catcher, Hit-and-Run Victim, Buried.*"

John McVey was reportedly a battery mate of Charles "Old Hoss" Radbourne (who, by the way, won sixty games in 1884 for the Providence Grays), according to the article, and "was a National League catcher back in the old barehanded days of the 80's and 90's. He played for Detroit, Cleveland, Providence, Pittsburgh, and Baltimore. McVey finished his major league career at Baltimore as John McGraw was starting his career with the famous minor league Orioles."

Verifying experience for guys who played in the 1880s is challenging, not impossible, but aside from this obit, I could find nothing that confirmed John McVey was telling the truth about his baseball career. His name fails to appear on what are surprisingly complete rosters of players from that era in several baseball references. I suspect but cannot prove that he was an early sufferer of Eddie Scissons Syndrome, in spite of the credibility he earned as a *hit-and-run* victim.

Triple-play King

Then there's the case of Sal Rizzo, which also took place prior to the advent of the Internet.

I received a letter from a friend at the Hall of Fame many years ago that revealed Sal was passing himself off as a member of the Boston Red Sox from 1932 to 1948. He claimed to hold the major league record for unassisted triple-plays with thirteen during his illustrious career, and Sal even stated he was "*nominated* for induction into the Baseball Hall of Fame."

By the way, as of this writing, only fifteen times in all of baseball history has a player fielded an unassisted triple play, making it rarer than a perfect game. And not one of those fifteen ever fielded more than one in his career. As a frame of reference,

Tris Speaker holds the major league record for turning the most unassisted double-plays during a career with six. Apparently, Sal Rizzo's obituary, while interesting and impressive, included some inaccuracies. Embellishments? No, just lies.

Chapter 13

ESS IN POPULAR CULTURE

To me, it's always surprising, disappointing even, when I discover a celebrity suffering from Eddie Scissons Syndrome. I always want that celebrity to be better than that, even if it's a politician I don't particularly care for, I want them to be better than that. Even if it's an actor I don't follow, I don't want to see him lying, outright lying! … on a talk show about having played a professional sport when I know he didn't. You have read some cases in the previous chapters of guys who accomplished so much in their lives, yet they felt the need to fabricate a baseball career to add to their list. Why? Isn't being elected President of the United States enough? Isn't winning an Emmy enough? Isn't being recognized and admired from almost everyone you pass by on the street, enough?

Five star general, supreme allied commander, war hero, US president… and a semi-professional baseball player?

Dwight Eisenhower loved baseball. The 34th United States president, as a boy, had a dream of playing professional baseball. As Eisenhower was once quoted, "When I was a small boy in

Kansas, a friend of mine and I went fishing. I told him I wanted to be a real Major League baseball player, a genuine professional like Honus Wagner. My friend said that he'd like to be President of the United States. Neither of us got our wish."

Ike never became a real Major League baseball player, and he failed to make West Point's baseball team. He did, however, briefly claim to have played semi-pro ball.

In June 1945, after he returned from World War II, he was celebrated at a Giants-Braves game at the Polo Grounds, and when asked about his baseball career, Eisenhower mentioned how he'd played in the Kansas State League under the assumed name of Wilson.

Asked what position, Eisenhower claimed "That's one of the secrets of my life."

That secret—centerfield—was revealed weeks later. But even then, details didn't quite add up. Junction City, the team Ike was suspected to play for, had a short-term player, "D. Wilson," in 1911 but wasn't in the Kansas State League that season.

Those who said they remembered him playing offered conflicting information. A fan, Elmer Twitchell, claimed in newspaper accounts that Eisenhower "played any and all positions" and that Ike "was a smart pitcher."

Did he play? Did he not play? Did he pitch? The truth is hazy.

And on top of that, getting paid to play baseball would have undermined his sterling West Point reputation and potentially gotten him disqualified.

After leaving the White House, Eisenhower—attempting to prevent additional information from leaking out—told his staff not to answer any inquiries involving his baseball career, "as it would necessarily become too complicated." Maybe… but with all that he accomplished, and the list is very long and beyond impressive, he still felt a need to add a mysterious *baseball career* to the conversation. Defeating the Nazis and keeping Americans from having to learn to speak German should be high on most people's list of why they respect and admire Dwight Eisenhower. I don't care that he never played centerfield for the Yankees… he was still a hero whose life was consequential and meaningful. Did he really need to add professional baseball to his resume?

Of course, President Eisenhower isn't the only U.S. president accused of puffing up or lying about his background. Former President Ronald Reagan very publicly recounted to a French Diplomat his own personal experience on D-Day, storming the beaches of Normandy.

Reagan also very publicly told then Israeli Prime Minister Yitzhak Shamir that one of the reasons why he was so heavily committed to Israel was because he had personally taken part in the liberation of the death camps, and will never forget the horrors he saw, and how it affected him so deeply.

Well, it's no secret and it's very well documented that Reagan never stormed the beaches of Normandy, never was personally involved in freeing the concentration camps, and he never set foot in Europe during World War II.

Memory is a tricky thing.

Reagan did make some patriotic movies during the war, and I suppose after a while, it may have been difficult for him to discern whether that was a war movie he made or a real war in which he actually fought. And he also played a fictionalized version of Grover Cleveland Alexander in the 1952 movie, *The Winning Team.* Hopefully, he understood why Grover Cleveland Alexander was in the Big Mac, and he was not.

President Reagan is a beloved historical figure by many people throughout the world, and I mean no disrespect, but these are facts. And yet, I think we might agree that if we compare Reagan's tall tales to those of twenty-first century politicians, he actually comes out looking pretty good.

James Caan

Actor James Caan appeared on NBC's *The Tonight Show* on November 18, 1977. He was plugging a new movie but spent most of his time talking about his personal athletic achievements, mostly bull-riding. During the conversation with host Johnny Carson, Caan also discussed his baseball career, his dreams—and near-glory.

"I guess 50% of the American male population over 40, they put themselves to sleep dreaming they've just struck out the Yankees," he said. "So, I always wanted to be a professional athlete. … I played a little Triple-A baseball. Never quite good enough," an answer he gave Johnny why he didn't *quite* make it to the Big Leagues. These comments were offensive for a variety of reasons, not the least of which because we know it takes tremendous dedication, skill and commitment among other attributes, for most ballplayers to actually reach Triple-A level. Diminishing that level of play is insulting to those many thousand minor leaguers who never make it to Triple-A, let alone the Big Leagues. And Caan claimed in later interviews to have been a "semi-pro infielder." What that means is still open for interpretation, but what we know is that none of it was true.

Caan did attempt to play football at Michigan State University, but he failed to make the team.

Nowhere in my research about the actor does there appear any reference to his having played at any level of professional baseball, semi or otherwise, let alone *a little Triple-A baseball.*

Caan was Sonny Corleone in *the Godfather*, he was novelist Paul Sheldon in *Misery*, he played in many of the greatest movies of his time. He was Brian Piccolo in *Brian's Song*, for crissakes! And if you haven't seen the 1975 classic movie, *Rollerball*, put this book down right now and find it somewhere streaming on your very own television. No need to thank me, just watch Rollerball, then get back to the book. My point is he was an accomplished, great actor, (and I can hear you screaming "what about this movie or that movie that James Caan starred in?" Hey, that's not the point, we're not debating which movie was his best! Do that on your own time!) My point is, he did not need to make up a minor league baseball career in which he was so close to making it to the show. We loved him even without that reference. And some of us might even have respected him more without it. But this ESS is a powerful force, and it grips even the most unlikely victims in its wake.

Caan did, however, maintain connections to the game. The lifelong Yankee fan coached his son Scott's Little League team during a break in acting. That appears to be the extent of it.

Wedding crashers

John Beckwith (Owen Wilson) and his pal Jeremy Grey (Vince Vaughn) present fake versions of themselves at weddings to get women to sleep with them in the 2005 comedy *Wedding Crashers*. One lie is more outrageous than the next, and in one scene, they show off fake Purple Hearts, indifferent about stolen military valor.

A montage shows the men repeating different lines to generate sympathy with women.

John mentions, on multiple occasions, about how we "lost so many good men out there."

One woman pulls back.

"Playing with the Yankees?" she asks him.

He commits to the lie. "Yes, with the Yankees. You lose good men to trades and unruly fans. I … look, I don't want to talk about it, I'm sorry."

Eddie Scissons Syndrome sufferers have been known to lie about their baseball careers to impress women, and in *Wedding Crashers* we see a humorous glimpse of ESS at the movies, nothing more.

Chapter 14

"PHANTOM PLAYERS"

Terminology matters when considering Major League players who weren't.

There's a reason why this book is titled "Baseball Imposters" and not "Phantom Players," as I had previously mis-labeled them. Imposters' careers were an apparition—they didn't exist. Phantom Players, as they are labeled by the Hall of Fame, worked their way up the ladder, only to fall short for a host of reasons. Most important are the key words, "worked their way up…" as Imposters have not "worked" at anything but lying, and some have perfected that art.

I first recognized the distinction when talking to Society for American Baseball Research (SABR) chair emeritus Bill Hickman. In conversation, I told Bill that I felt "Phantom Players" deserve our condemnation, not understanding the difference.

As it turns out, the term "Phantom Players," as Bill Hickman and other insiders use it, describes players who were called up to the major league team without making it into a game. Bill has maintained a file for SABR, with thousands of names of phantom players who wore a major league uniform, sat in the dugout or out in the bullpen among other major leaguers, traveled with the team on the same plane, stayed at the same hotels, ate at the same restaurants, and lived the life of a major league baseball player… maybe for a day, a week, a couple weeks, but never made it into a game. There are well known cases of players being brought up to pitch a game, giving the tired pitching staff a break during the long season, perhaps due to injuries or other temporary setbacks… but because of weather or injury, they were not used, were sent back to the minor leagues, never to return.

True "Phantom Players" aren't lying, and they didn't fictionalize their big league callups. They were on the major league roster, during the season, or possibly during Spring Training. They were in uniform and they traveled with the team. They came as close as you can get, but never made it into the record books. And I'm pretty certain that few, if any, claim that stolen baseball valor by lying about it, by telling people they are former major leaguers… understanding the difference, and the gravity of what it takes to be a major league baseball player. Their story is interesting enough, and their career is marked by hard work, great baseball skills and the achievements they made in their minor league careers. Sometimes luck plays a part, or in many cases involving Phantom Players, bad luck.

Bill Hickman maintains a database of "near major leaguers" online that features players who made Major League rosters during the regular season but did not appear in a game; players who made spring rosters but did not appear in a Major League game; and non-roster invitees to spring training who did not appear in a Major League game. There are more than 8,000 players in Bill's database.

As Hickman suggests, the database shows just how many minor leaguers "creep right up to the edge of Big League status, but for one reason or another never make it into a game and thus never get their names into the record books."

The Bill Sharman Society

Broadcaster and baseball historian Keith Olbermann coined the term "the Bill Sharman Society" in appreciation of the most famous Phantom Player, who spent two weeks on the Dodgers' roster in 1951, but didn't appear in a game—and never returned to the big leagues—before becoming a star for the NBA's Boston Celtics.

Some attention for the Phantom Players

This class of near major leaguers called phantom players have gotten some visibility over the years.

In 2018, *Washington Post* columnist Dave Sheinin wrote about the "star-crossed, largely obscure minor leaguers who, in one way or another, were promoted to the majors but never appeared in a Big League game." He gave the example of Ryan Bollinger, who was called up for a day by the Yankees but returned to the Trenton Thunder (a Double-A minor league team) without appearing in the game. He also told of the sad tale of Phillies farmhand Brian Mazone, who was called up from Triple-A to pitch against the Houston Astros, but after the game was rained out, he was sent back because the Phillies no longer needed him, and so his only shot at the Big Leagues got rained out.

Neither Bollinger nor Mazone appear in the Big Mac or any major league register because they never entered a major league game.

Here are a few other notable "Phantom" Players.

Phantom Player Chet Trail

A "designated player," Trail spent the 1964 season on the Yankees roster despite playing in the minors—a chance for the team to maintain his rights. Since he was on the roster all season, the Yankees were required to keep him on the roster for the World Series, even though Trail hadn't spent a day during the regular season with the club. He retired after the 1969 season, never having played in the major leagues, and later became a pastor.

Phantom Player Brian Jeroloman

Jeroloman, a catcher, was called up in 2011 by the Blue Jays. But his timing couldn't have been worse—he'd just broken his hand. Despite spending 37 days with the team, he didn't make it into a game. Even so, he was making the most of the opportunity and "studying non-stop," lessons that would come in handy years later as Jeroloman shifted from Phantom Player to professional baseball coach.

Phantom Player Jesus Martinez

You may have heard of the Martinez brothers, star pitchers Pedro and Ramon. Jesus Martinez was called up by the Dodgers in 1996—the first time since the Alous in 1974 that three brothers were in the majors at the same time—but unlike his siblings, he never pitched in an MLB game. His pro career lasted from 1992 until 2001.

Phantom Player Bill Merrifield

Bill Merrifield was stuck. There was a logjam in the Angels system, and the infielder was mired in Triple A. He wanted a trade, and late in the 1987 season, he finally got his wish, getting moved to the Pirates. He got summoned to Pittsburgh to work out with the parent club for a few days, but that was as close as he'd come to appearing in a big league game. His son Whit fared better, getting selected for three All-Star games and spending the bulk of his nine-year MLB career with the Royals.

Phantom Player Les Hinckle

Hinckle was a standout minor league and semi-pro pitcher of the 1930s and early 1940s. His best baseball highlight came in 1938, when he pitched an exhibition game against the Phillies and won 2-1, a performance dubbed by one local newspaper as "probably the greatest pitching exhibition ever seen in this vicinity." Hinckle's contract was purchased by the Cincinnati Reds in 1941 but before he could make the team, he was injured in a car crash and never pitched in a major league game.

Chapter 15

LIES, LIES, AND MORE LIES

There are lots of others in and around the game who lied about their backgrounds, age, or other details. Let's explore some of the most explosive and notorious examples.

Tim Johnson

Tim Johnson wanted to motivate players.

The former player turned coach, then manager had served in the Marine reserves during the Vietnam War, but he never served overseas—instead, he was playing baseball.

Johnson used fake combat stories to inspire his players and he later claimed he felt it gave him added credibility with the press and with the fans. When he began coaching with the Boston Red Sox, he regaled players with details of the war in Vietnam from his perspective. Later, when managing the Blue Jays in 1998, Johnson shared the horrific details of a firefight in which he claimed to have participated, inadvertently killing several children among the villagers who died at the hands of his unit.

He led Toronto to a respectable 88-74 record that season,

but as the season wore on, the questions about Johnson's war stories grew louder as the lies unraveled. Following the season, he admitted that he hadn't been in Vietnam at all.

"There's been a lot of guilt," he said. "I've lost a lot of great friends that were in Vietnam, who were killed or wounded or missing in action or were a POW. There are a lot of things I said. I'm sorry for saying it. I can't dwell on it. We have all made mistakes."

He also lied about being offered a basketball scholarship at UCLA.

The controversy didn't go away, and the Blue Jays fired Johnson the following March during Spring Training when it became apparent the stories about his fake military career were a distraction. Veteran manager Jim Fregosi was hired to replace Johnson weeks before Opening Day.

Craig Calcaterra's take on this…

I start each day with a *Cup of Coffee*, the name of the daily newsletter from one of my favorite sportswriters, Craig Calcaterra. If you're a baseball fan (even if you're not a baseball fan!) and you're not a subscriber to *Cup of Coffee*, you are missing out, my friend.[11]

So much has been written about this Tim Johnson spectacle, but for me, what Calcaterra wrote about it on March 17, 2016, puts it all in perspective.

That day, Calcaterra's piece commemorated the seventeenth anniversary of the Blue Jays firing Johnson. From Calcaterra:

"While it's hard not to have at least some sympathy for Johnson—he had suicidal thoughts at times after he was disgraced—Johnson's wounds were entirely self-inflicted. Lying about military service is extraordinarily low and disrespectful of those who served and, especially, those who faced combat and those who died (and their families). Sympathy, sure. Understanding and forgiveness is another matter entirely, especially from those who did serve and those whose Johnson's lies impacted.

"The dynamic of how small lies turn into big ones is pretty well understood. You get a benefit from the lie and want to get more so you enhance your lie. At some point the lie is so big it's impossible to backtrack unless and until you're caught in it. The specific dynamic of military imposter lying is less well-understood, but it's not entirely inexplicable. Johnson said it began with his guilt over people he trained with going off to war while he went off to play baseball with a coveted reserve slot. It's obvious, of course, that over time he enhanced his lies for more selfish

---

[11] https://www.cupofcoffeenews.com/

reasons of self-aggrandizement and, indirectly anyway, career enhancement as a war story-telling coach."[12]

See what I mean about Craig Calcaterra? This guy can write!

Catching a guy who is lying about having played major league baseball is much easier than exposing the lie of stolen military valor because of technological advances, and because there is no Big Mac or Baseball-Reference.com for those who served. But it makes you wonder what else is out there. Who else is telling us lies that we never saw coming, or passing themselves off as someone they are not?

Al Martin

After Mariners outfielder Al Martin collided with a teammate, Carlos Guillen, during a 2001 game, he compared it to a run-in during his football days playing for USC.

"For some reason, probably because I was young and dumb, I decided I could make a head-on stop of (Michigan's) Leroy Hoard," Martin told the Seattle Times. "I hit him, or rather he hit me. You remember those big tree-trunk legs Hoard had? That's what hit me."[13]

But USC didn't play Michigan in the year Martin claimed. And as it turned out, Martin didn't play football at USC—a lie Martin had passed off throughout his MLB career.

The Mariners media guide claimed that Martin "played two

[12] Calcaterra, Craig. "Remembering the Ignominious End to Tim Johnson's Managerial Career." *NBC Sports*, 17 Mar. 2016, www.nbcsports.com/mlb/news/remembering-the-ignominious-end-to-tim-johnsons-managerial-career.

[13] "Looks Like Al Martin Never Played at USC." *The Seattle Times*, 28 Aug. 2001, archive.seattletimes.com/archive/20010828/mart28/looks-like-al-martin-never-played-at-usc.

seasons at strong safety for the Trojans."

Martin, when confronted about the discrepancies, said he would provide proof. He never did, because there wasn't any. The team quietly removed the erroneous information from future media guides.

You'd think Martin would have learned. But his later biographical info when he played for the Devil Rays in 2003 claimed he was named to the 1994 All-Star team but did not play due to a sprained wrist.

When confronted about the All-Star flim-flam, Martin suggested that Joe Torre was the team's manager (it was actually Jim Fregosi) and claimed it was down to him or Pirates teammate Carlos Garcia (Garcia actually was chosen for the game).

"I wasn't on the team. I got selected. I got chosen, not selected in '94. Carlos Garcia went to that game," he told Mike Berardino of the South Florida Sun-Sentinel.

Huh? Martin's injury happened just before the July 12 game … or about a week *after* Garcia had already been named to the team.

Bill "Spaceman" Lee

During Spring Training 1989, my boss's boss, Dr. Richard Astro asked me to accompany him to Winter Haven to see a Red Sox spring training game. I couldn't say no. He was the Provost and I was just a shlub Associate Director of Admissions at the time, but we were both baseball fans. So, I went with him and gave a presentation about the college admissions process to the entire roster of Boston Red Sox players at all levels, about ninety players in Red Sox uniforms, along with several support staff, offering to help them with an opportunity to start or finish their college degrees.

Many had started college but had never completed their degrees, which was especially common for players who traveled throughout much of the year. This was long before distance-learning became a thing, and way before the Internet came into being and changed everything… especially in the way of higher educational opportunities for everyone, including athletes who are unable to stay in one place long enough to earn a degree.

For professional athletes, there were few opportunities to work on completion of a college degree anywhere. Guys like Richard Astro at UCF worked to change that, a credit to his foresight in leading the charge when the easy answer was *too bad, either come to class or finish your degree when you retire from baseball. Sorry, that's just the way it is.*

So Rich Astro initiated a program enabling us to offer help with admission to Northeastern University for players who made the big club in Boston. For Triple-A players in Pawtucket, we offered courses through the University of Rhode Island if they met URI admissions standards. Those assigned to Winter Haven in the Florida State League could attend our university, UCF in Orlando, if they were academically qualified. We reviewed their copies of grade reports and transcripts if they brought them to the meeting, having been told in advance that this service would be available.

A few guys stayed behind after the presentation, not many, but a few who had accumulated a number of college credits and inquired about what it would take to finish. One guy who stayed after the meeting ended was Bill Lee, from somewhere other than Planet Earth. "The Spaceman," as he was called due to his unorthodox and entertaining way of thinking and behaving, (and maybe because we all know there is superior intelligence on other planets!), joined in our conversation with then General Manager Lou Gorman. Noticing the large stack of UCF catalogs I was lugging,

Lee told us he had attended UCF in the mid-1970s, taking one course toward completion of his degree from the University of Southern California. It seemed plausible. At his request, I proudly handed him a catalog which I suspect found its way into the trash before he stepped back on to the diamond later that day.

Sadly, when I returned to campus, I checked our university's Big Mac, the UCF *Ever Attend* book. No one by the name of William Francis Lee Jr. ever attended our school, or had ever applied for admission, or had ever requested a transcript for the work he completed at UCF to be sent to USC. *What did this mean?* I wondered. Was it an honest mistake? Did he confuse us with another university? Is this one of the reasons why they call him "The Spaceman?" Is this a new strain of ESS? *Spaceman Syndrome…a tendency of former professional athletes to claim they attended the University of Central Florida.* Are there variations of this phenomenon in other localities? How many other universities have been affected by this new strain? Is this cause for alarm for admissions professionals at colleges across the country?

In his defense, Bill Lee was really fun to be around, interesting, entertaining, and respectful. I have no explanation why he claimed to have attended UCF. He had not attended, but I wish he had. He would have made us proud. Bill Lee is one of the great characters of the game, and if the worst thing you can say about him is that he said he attended UCF when he hadn't, well, I say welcome to the UCF Alumni Association! I'll campaign for your honorary membership.

Another name for Jack Benny syndrome?

Lying about one's age to increase a player's value is fairly common among prospects from Latin America. Baseball is an avenue to rescue a family from poverty, and players—or their relatives—have taken drastic measures in order to increase their chances of getting discovered. Here are some of the most notorious examples.

Danny Almonte

Danny Almonte didn't look like the other 12-year-old boys. He was bigger and more developed. And his pitches were a blur.

The Little League sensation led his Bronx team to a third place finish in the 2001 Little League World Series. He pitched a perfect game and struck out 62 of the 72 batters he faced.

Following the series, it was revealed that Almonte's father had falsified his records—he was actually 14, not 12. Allegedly, Danny himself had no idea about the falsified documents.

He later played college and semi-pro baseball before becoming a coach at the high school level.

Wandy Rodriguez

Wandy Rodriguez was 19 years old, throwing in the mid-80s—which wasn't enough to get him noticed by pro scouts. A 17-year-old, on the other hand, would get noticed … so Rodriguez used his friend's identity and called himself Eny Cabreja, (coincidentally, the same name I used in Hebrew School as a kid).

Wandy lived with that lie for four years before finally telling the Astros the truth. He was fortunate the Astros didn't send him back to the Dominican Republic. By then, they had realized his potential. But had Wandy not used the identity of Eny Cabreja, he probably would have never had the chance to play in America.

Miguel Tejada

Miguel Tejada, Dominican shortstop, played sixteen years in the Big Leagues predominantly with the Oakland A's and the Baltimore Orioles. He won the AL MVP in 2002. He had also lied about his age. Claiming his birthday was May 25, 1976, instead of 1974, goes back to when he first signed a major league contract in 1993. When ESPN reporter Tom Farrey confronted Tejada in 2008 with his actual birth certificate, he stormed out of the interview. By then, of course, this was all past history and there was nothing to be done.

It certainly is apparent *why* these guys would lie about their age. They lied for a chance for a better life. And while lying about only two years doesn't seem to be that big a deal, it's still a lie. Like with Wandy Rodriguez, that 2 years made a big difference to his employer.

Adrian Beltre

Not all players lie to appear younger—some lie to appear older.

That was the case with Hall of Fame third baseman Adrian Beltre, who was only 15 years old—not 16, the minimum age—when the Dodgers signed him in 1994.

The truth came to light in 1999, after Beltre's agent, Scott Boras, took the matter to the league. Beltre and Boras claimed that Los Angeles knew the player was underage when they signed him.

The Dodgers were fined $50,000, ordered to pay Beltre $48,500, and forced to shut down their Dominican baseball operation for one year.

Cesar Altagracia

The Padres reached a verbal agreement with one of the top teenage prospects in the Dominican Republic, Cesar Altagracia, thinking the player was 14 years old. He was actually 19.

Had the deal kicked in, San Diego would have signed the player for a $4 million bonus when he became eligible to sign as a 16-year-old international free agent.

The agreement was withdrawn when the truth came to light in 2024, and the end result is that Altagracia is not and has never been a household name throughout baseball loving America.

Stand-ins and imposters

Over the years, non-players have assumed identities of players with their permission, to sign autographs, make public appearances, conduct interviews, and more. (Shame on them!) Andre Dawson and Tim Raines had stand-ins provided by the Expos during the 1982 pennant race. These stand-ins were in some cases trained actors, given enough knowledge of their players to give credible interviews. And in some cases, stand-ins were actual players. Carl Boles, a reserve outfielder, was called up in 1962 by the San Francisco Giants and appeared in 19 games—but his main purpose was serving as an autograph alter-ego for Willie Mays.

As Boles lamented in one interview, "If I could've traded the looks for the swing, I'd be making $105,000 a year. I signed baseballs and programs for him, but he signed his own checks."[14]

Reportedly, Jose Cardenal played a similar role for Orlando Cepeda in 1963.

I call these imposter shenanigans distant cousins to lying about

---

[14] George Ross, "A Giant in Town." *Oakland Tribune*, March 3, 1965.

playing in the Big Leagues… but in the strictest sense, Boles and guys like him are not considered Baseball Imposters. Still, it's a shameful practice and should be called out.

The curious case of Sidd Finch

The tale was too good to be true. A mythical, eccentric, Tibet-trained, French horn-playing, one-booted Mets pitching prospect throwing the ball 168 miles an hour.

George Plimpton's account of the Mets mystery man graced the pages of the April 1, 1985, issue of *Sports Illustrated*.

The article featured quotes and insights from numerous baseball figures, including then-commissioner Peter Ueberroth. "I'll have to see it to believe it!" he told the publication.

We all did … which was the point. The article was a hoax. There was no Sidd Finch. Eagle-eyed readers recognized the charade by reading the first letters of the article's subhead: "Happy April Fool's Day."

Chapter 16

ESS IN OTHER VENUES

While this book has focused on lying in baseball, Eddie Scissons Syndrome isn't unique to the sport. Let's explore some of examples of people lying about their background or qualifications in other avenues.

George O'Leary

There was a palpable excitement when George O'Leary was hired as Notre Dame's head football coach in late 2001.

He'd found success at Georgia Tech. The Yellow Jackets, under O'Leary's guidance, became one of the country's top offensive teams.

But within days of being hired, it emerged that O'Leary had fabricated elements of his resume, and he tendered his resignation.

The lies were unearthed when Jim Fennell, a sportswriter for the Union Leader in Manchester, New Hampshire, began working on a story about O'Leary's collegiate career. His bio stated that he'd lettered three times.

But it turned out, he hadn't even played on the team.

After the reporter reached out to Notre Dame for comment

about the discrepancy, officials with Notre Dame started asking questions.

O'Leary initially brushed off the discrepancy. Maybe a sports information staffer puffed up his credentials. The Notre Dame officials followed up by asking if anything else in the coach's background didn't line up, and O'Leary voluntarily admitted that he hadn't completed his master's degree.

With that, O'Leary chose to resign.

"Many years ago, as a young married father, I sought to pursue my dream as a football coach. In seeking employment, I prepared a resume that contained inaccuracies regarding my completion of coursework for a master's degree and also my level of participation in football at my Alma Mater," he said in a statement. "These misstatements were never stricken from my resume or biographical sketch in later years."

I love the passive voice that always seems to accompany statements like these… "These misstatements were never stricken…," not "I never removed these statements…." This is common among liars who finally come forward, they just can't bring themselves to saying "I did this, or I didn't do what I should have done…" instead of making some vague statement that almost blames someone else who should have taken care of this. It's rare to find exceptions to this rule in the ESS world.

Despite the scandal, O'Leary was able to pick up his coaching career, first as an assistant coach with the NFL's Minnesota Vikings, and later as the head coach at the University of Central Florida, where he did a fabulous job building UCF's program, and the people associated with UCF loved him. I was a proud, active alumnus and former long-time employee at the time O'Leary was hired. My thinking? *Notre Dame's standards apparently don't apply to us.*

O'Leary was a great coach whose bounce-back shows us a pathway forward for those who get caught lying or puffing up their credentials. He led with contrition, owned the mistake (sort-of), and basically took responsibility for it. There really wasn't much else he could do at that point. And it helped that he knew how to win.

The Case of Joseph P. Ellis

The academic world was rocked in 2001 when Joseph P. Ellis, a longtime, respected history professor and Pulitzer Prize-winning author, was revealed to have lied about his exploits in the Vietnam War. There actually weren't any exploits, because he had never been in Vietnam.

As it turned out, Ellis had told many lies about his background:

- He claimed to have been a paratrooper in Vietnam, a member of the staff of General William Westmoreland in Saigon, and said he was interviewed by David Halberstam for the book "The Best and Brightest."

- He embellished his role in the Civil Rights and anti-war movements.

- Not to be outdone, Ellis also claimed to have scored the winning touchdown in an important high school football game while there is no record of him playing sports in high school.

The lies came to light when a tip was passed to the Boston Globe's Spotlight team. Reporter Walter Robinson pursued the story and unraveled Ellis' many false claims.

The act of lying about one's military service is shameful and sadly, not uncommon. What made Ellis' situation notable was his success as a professor at Mount Holyoke College and as a high-profile, well respected author.

Ellis wrote the Jefferson biography *American Sphinx* for which he won the 1997 National Book Award, and later *Founding Brothers: The Revolutionary Generation* which won the Pulitzer Prize and was a bestseller for 26 weeks.

The lies were not only perplexing, but they also cast a shadow over Ellis' many accomplishments. What could one believe about his historical work? Could his fabrications from his personal life and teaching also bleed into his research and writing?

"By misrepresenting my military service to students in the course on the Vietnam War, I did something both stupid and wrong," he said in a statement issued after his lies were exposed. "I apologize to the students, as well as to the faculty of this institution, for violating the implicit covenant of trust that must exist in the classroom. Finally, I apologize to those Vietnam veterans who have expressed their understandable anger about my lie. I am truly sorry for the hurt I have caused."[15]

This is how apologies should look, not that passive, fake language that implies it's someone else's fault. Maybe Professor Ellis should teach a course on admitting to shameful lies.

Ellis was suspended without pay for a year and later returned to the classroom, but he was prohibited from teaching a course on the 1960s, since most of his lies centered around that decade.[16]

What ESS researchers can learn from Frank Deford

Legendary sports columnist, editor and correspondent Frank

---

[15] Ellis, Joseph J. *"Further Statement of Joseph J. Ellis."* Mount Holyoke College, 17 Aug. 2001. Web Archive, archived 15 July 2006, web.archive.org/web/20060715135033/http://www.mtholyoke.edu/offices/comm/news/ellisstatement.htm.

[16] Marshall, John. "Ellis Doesn't Want to Revisit His Own Past." *Seattle Post-Intelligencer,* 6 Dec. 2004, www.seattlepi.com/entertainment/books/article/Ellis-doesnt-want-to-revisit-his-own-past-1161328.php.

Deford wrote a piece in 1995 that I've kept for over thirty years. It really captured the essence of ESS, in spite of not being related to baseball.

DeFord's wife read an obituary of a former college classmate, Adam Douglas, Olympian, who, it said, played in two Olympics and captained the American team. She knew him back then as a mediocre player on a subpar college soccer squad.

Deford checked the records and found the U.S. had not even qualified for Olympic Soccer during those years Adam Douglas claimed to have played.

A soccer expert in the area who Frank knew laughed. "I remember Adam," he said. "One year he was a hanger-on for the Pan-Am team because he would pay his own way." The expert went on, "you can't imagine how many members of the Czech national team or Bulgarian national team have soccer jobs in the United States. About a thousand a team."

Deford chuckled, remembering how once when he was writing a story about the Harlem Globetrotters, he played against them in Bologna, and had himself introduced as a former All-American from Villanova, an especially nice touch for his new Italian fans.

This was different to Deford, it was a "transparent gag" … and the Czechs and Bulgarians only pumped up their resumes specifically to get good jobs in America. But there was no money in Adam Douglas' fraud. Deford wondered, "Why would the man do it?"

The rest of this piece is why I saved it more than thirty years ago.

"I went back to the obituary. He had been married a second time, moved, was raising a second family. His first family would have known he was just a scrub at soccer, at all athletics. But his second family—ah, how proud they must have been for Daddy to have been an Olympic captain.

"Why?" I wondered. Why did Adam feel the need to create this fiction? Is it just that sports defines us so? Did he tell the story once, idly, and watch it grow over time? Or did he plan the tale, and then consciously elaborate on it? Did he ever fear what a fool he would be if one night at a cocktail party some real soccer player said: are you kidding me? Or did he worry: how his little boy would feel then? or his wife?

"And more, I wondered: we are a nation of men who have moved, with second wives and second families. How many other American soccer captains are out there, still living in Orange County, or in Phoenix, or Seattle, or Boise? How many thousands of All-Americans are out there? State Champions? Nos. 1? Olympians? Olympic captains? How many of us men have lied about the playing fields of long ago in order to dress up our humdrum lives and impress the people we fear might not love us so much just for ourselves?

"Adam Douglas must have told his Olympic lie so many times that he understood that he would be identified with it in death. He probably felt no shame or fear of discovery any longer because probably by now he believed all that himself. If every week on SportsZone, I was introduced as 'Frank Deford, All-American from Villanova, 'I guess even I would believe that by now.'"

Frank Deford, a Princeton graduate, class of 1962, died in 2017 at the age of 78. He had an incredibly impressive resume with a list of well-earned awards and achievements that would fill many pages of this book. Six times he was voted by his peers as Sportswriter of the Year. Frank's column is a good reminder why he was so decorated for his work. I like this column because it shows his ability to dig deeper in capturing the complexities of the human spirit and ultimately the Eddie Scissons Syndrome.

Chapter 17

NOT ALL IMPOSTERS
ARE HARMLESS

S ome baseball imposters are more sinister than others.

It's one thing for someone to falsely claim that they played Major League Baseball. It's something else entirely—and something much more shameful—to falsely claim a baseball player's identity.

Let's look at some of the strangest cases of baseball imposters—those who passed themselves off as actual players.

Two-faced

Yankee teammates Julie Wera and Babe Ruth combined to hit 61 home runs in 1927.

The Sultan of Swat slugged sixty. Wera, a backup third baseman, smashed his only career home run during a Fourth of July game against the Washington Senators, a 21-1 blowout win.

Wera also appeared with the Yankees in 1929 before settling into domestic life. He became a butcher at a Piggly Wiggly meat market in Minnesota, and there wasn't much that was notable about Wera's post-playing days until 1948.

That year, an imposter claiming to be Wera talked his way into becoming a business manager and scout for the Red Sox farm club in Oroville, California. Making the situation even stranger? Some of Wera's former teammates were even fooled, as the imposter claimed that a mine blew off his face during World War II and he had plastic surgery—thus, the altered appearance.

The situation only came to light when the imposter—later identified as William James Werra (also spelled Wera)—died of an overdose of sleeping pills.

A counterfeit Bill

Everyone who knew Bill Henry liked him. The Lakeland, Florida man had stories. When you spend 16 years in the majors as a reliever and pitch in the World Series, you rack up lots of tales.

Bill was a good guy to be around. But when Bill died in 2007 at the age of 83, a stunning discovery came to light—the man who'd spent decades passing himself off as Bill Henry, former relief pitching ace, was a different Bill Henry, one who'd never played in the big leagues. Both men looked similar, both were lefthanded, both were 6'2" and both were named Bill Henry.

The *actual baseball playing* Bill Henry was alive and well in Texas and surprised when he heard the *news* about his death. The retired pitcher wasn't angry about *counterfeit Bill*, rather, he was more impressed than anything else.

"It's amazing that a guy could pull a hoax for that long, isn't it?" he told Sports Illustrated's Rick Reilly. "I'd congratulate him. If that's what the guy needed to do to help his career, it don't bother me… I just hope they don't stop my Social Security."[17]

---

[17] Reilly, Rick. "The Passing of a Counterfeit Bill." *Sports Illustrated*, 24 Sept. 2007, vault.si.com/vault/2007/09/24/the-passing-of-a-counterfeit-bill.

Bleacher seats? Really?

In 1983, a man who resembled Phillies shortstop Ivan DeJesus was arrested and charged with three counts of first degree theft, running up debts of nearly $30,000 while posing as DeJesus.

Oscar A. DeJesus, no relation to Ivan, met a woman at a Honolulu disco in 1981 and later moved in with her. He was accused of borrowing $25,000 from the woman's father and getting $3,000 worth of dental work done by two Honolulu dentists—he then asked the dentists to send the bills to the Phillies (the team did not pay the bills).

When asked to explain why he remained in Hawaii for two years while the Phillies went through their regular season, he replied that "it was part of his contract that another player would fill in for him under his name and use his uniform," according to police detectives working the case.

Oscar even took the woman and her father to a Giants-Phillies game at Candlestick Park and made them sit high up in the bleachers while he supposedly went to play in the game, according to Detective Michael Orian. "The real DeJesus was hurt in the chest during the game and afterwards, Oscar told the girl and her father his chest was sore."

But to me, the real question is… What good is it to have a friend or a spouse playing for a major league team if they can't get you better seats than that?

Will the real Nick Eddy please stand…

Nick Eddy played five seasons with the Detroit Lions after an All-American college career at the University of Notre Dame. He was a finalist for the Heisman Trophy and led his Fighting Irish team to a national championship in 1966. After a long, successful career as an insurance executive, Eddy went back to school to earn a teaching certificate, and now 81-years old, he had a second career as a Special Education teacher in Modesto, California. With four grown children, nine grandchildren and a job that he loved, Nick Eddy has led an exemplary life. So, it makes sense that someone would want to be *be* him.

It turns out, William McMullen did, and for more than 20 years, he impersonated Eddy, serving as assistant football coach at Old Colony Regional Vocational Technical High School in Rochester, Massachusetts. McMullen got away with the impersonation until the school received a call from the real Nick Eddy, ending McMullen's coaching career in 1999.

"It's so bizarre, so silly," Eddy said at the time. "I'm not sure how I should react. At first I was angry. How could this guy impersonate me? As I get more details, I can't feel sorry for him because he got himself into it. But I feel great empathy for his wife and his in-laws who think he is Nick Eddy."[18]

---

[18] Agostini, Ron. "Great Pretender." *The Modesto Bee*, 7 Oct. 1999, p. A1.

Chapter 18

THREE DIFFERENT "COZY" DOLANS

The obituary for William Dolan, dated November 18, 1986, states he was ninety-six, so he would have been born in 1890. It reports "William 'Cozy' Dolan, who spent most of his life in Tonawanda, New York, died November 13 in Poway, California. Born in West Port, Connecticut. He had lived in Poway since 1978."

It went on to say, "He pitched for the Detroit Tigers of the American League and played on a number of minor league teams from 1908–1914." The curious part comes next. The obit stated "he later coached baseball at St. Bonaventure University and at the University of Buffalo. During the off-season, he was a featured singer in vaudeville, in upstate New York and Canada. He retired from the Buffalo Bolt Company in Tonawanda in 1955."

None of that profile information overlaps with any of the information available for either of the *two* Cozy Dolans who did play major league baseball.

According to Baseball-Reference.com and Google searches, Patrick Henry "Cozy" Dolan was a baseball player who played from 1895 to 1906. He was born in Cambridge, Massachusetts, and died in Louisville, Kentucky. He played as a right fielder, first baseman, and pitcher. There's no information connecting him to St. Bonaventure University in any capacity.

The other "Cozy Dolan" likely refers to Albert James "Cozy" Dolan, a former Major League Baseball player and coach. He played for several teams in the early twentieth century and later became a coach for the New York Giants. In 1924, he was banned from baseball for life after attempting to bribe a player to throw a game. This Cozy Dolan was an outfielder and third baseman who played for the Cincinnati Reds, New York Highlanders (later Yankees), Philadelphia Phillies, Pittsburgh Pirates, and Boston Braves.

While coaching for the New York Giants in 1924, he offered a bribe to Heinie Sand, a shortstop for the Phillies, to intentionally lose a game, according to baseball history websites. Sand reported the incident, and after an investigation, Commissioner Kennesaw Mountain Landis banned Dolan from baseball for life. In 1922, he made a brief appearance as a pinch runner for the Giants, seven years after his last major league game. But this Cozy Dolan, (Albert James Dolan), like the other Cozy Dolan, (Patrick Henry Dolan), was also never a coach for either St. Bonaventure University or the University of Buffalo.

So, what is going on here? We have two Cozy Dolans who played major league baseball but never played or coached at St. Bonaventure University. One played from 1895–1906 (Patrick Henry Dolan). The other (Albert James Dolan), played from 1909 to 1922, before joining the Giants as a coach, and being banned from baseball in 1924.

As it turned out, there was a third Dolan, a standout St. Bonaventure pitcher who, in 1912, was signed by the Detroit Tigers and pitched for Scranton of the New York State League, along with a handful of other minor league teams.

I contacted St. Bonaventure and Dennis Frank, St. Bonaventure's University Archivist, confirmed to me that William H. Dolan was connected to the school during that time period. As Dennis wrote, "I went back to the hard copy and found that William Dolan did, indeed, serve as our baseball coach for two years in 1914 and 1915. He came to Bona's in 1909 and pitched on the College Reserve team (the junior varsity) in 1908/09, then for the main squad from 1909/10-1911/12. He was not listed on the team in 1912/13, then came back as coach in 1913/14-1914/15." Notably, Dolan was referred to as "Cozy" in some newspaper reports from the time period.

The case of William Dolan really shows how difficult it can be sometimes to uncover the actual truth. Three men, three distinct baseball careers, all going by the same nickname. Lots of confusion and many man (people?) hours of research invested for a simple explanation. I suspect little Billy Dolan was called "Cozy"

as a young boy, because, how cute! He had the same last name as these big league ballplayers. Over time, the legend grew, one thing led to another and people just assumed this guy was Cozy Dolan, former major leaguer. He was pretty good, good enough to play for SBU, and later coach them, but he did not play major league baseball. He may not even be the culprit who claimed he did, but things like this can get out of control very easily. Maybe don't blame William but blame those who wanted him to be *that* Cozy Dolan!

Chapter 19
NOT EVERYONE IS A LIAR

On occasion, one of these guys tells a baseball story that turns out to be absolutely true. When that happens, it is quite exciting even though that guy is refused entry into the Eddie Scissons Hall of Fame. Here are some of my favorite examples.

Hal King

Whenever I saw Hal King around campus, he greeted me with a big wave and a friendly smile. Stopping to exchange pleasantries with Hal was consistently a positive experience and well worth the time and effort; he always seemed to be in a happy mood, in spite of the brutal heat and humidity he endured when sometimes his assignment called for working outdoors. Hal was a painter in the maintenance department at the University of Central Florida where I worked for many years, and one day he walked past my office carrying a tall ladder, apparently on the job. He did a double-take and stopped in to say hello. Noticing my baseball décor, Hal casually told me he had played baseball professionally. When asked more about it, he revealed that as a teenager, he played for the Indianapolis Clowns of the Negro Leagues.

"We had more fun than any circus clowns," he told me. He also casually mentioned playing for the Houston Astros and Cincinnati Reds as well as some other teams. It sounded legitimate, but I'd been burned so many times already. I didn't know what to believe anymore. While he looked like an athlete, that topic never came up previously in our brief conversations around campus.

I immediately looked him up as he watched me flipping through pages of the Big Mac, and sure enough, there was his name, "Harold (Hal) King!" Hal actually *was* a back-up catcher to Johnny Bench! Who would have thought? A nicer, humbler guy than Hal King would be hard to find.

For years after that encounter, Hal would put his ladder up against the wall, walk past the secretary who served as a literal gatekeeper at the front desk, and enter my office without notice. It didn't matter if I was in a meeting or on the phone, if I was with a prospective student and their family or just actually working! Hal would quietly march his colleagues in without warning, to show them page 1223 (where I kept a bookmark to speed up the transaction). He was just so proud to have his name and brief baseball statistical recap in print. I was proud of Hal and always felt his recognition was well earned, and it always brought out a broad smile as he pointed out his reference in the Big Mac to a colleague in the maintenance department.

Hal and I naturally lost touch after I left UCF when I moved to Los Angeles, and in 2019, I was sad to learn that Hal had died at the age of 75.

"Bud" Sketchley is in the book!

A few years ago, my neighbor, Rosemary, casually told me her father played major league baseball. She wasn't bragging, just stating a fact that had relevance in the context of our conversation. We were probably talking about what our fathers did during The War to keep us from having to learn to speak German, or worse… I suspected she was lying—yet another case of a Syndrome suffer-er—but sure enough, I looked it up on my phone in her presence, and Harry "Bud" Sketchley got seven hits in thirty-six at bats for the 1942 war-torn Chicago White Sox.

Interestingly enough, Sketchley had made the jump from UCLA to the majors without first playing in the minor leagues—Chicago's outfield was decimated with injuries and many players were away serving in the military. Sketchley started the season with the parent club in 1942.

That May, as rosters were trimmed down to 25 players, Sketchley was shipped to Waterloo to get more experience, never to return to the Big Leagues.

The 1942 season would be his first and only year playing or-ganized ball. But he in fact, played major league baseball.

President Korcheck was indeed a Senators back-up catcher

Dr. Steve Korcheck stopped by my office one afternoon at UCF during the mid-1980s and introduced himself as President of Manatee Community College. He was on campus for a state-wide meeting of college and university presidents and someone recommended that he stop by my baseball memorabilia-filled office. He came down to the first floor of the Administration Building to see for himself.

I didn't know anything about him but being told he was a college president gained him some credibility with me because I worked in that business, and showing respect to college presidents seemed like a good idea.

When Steve told me he had been a backup catcher with the Washington Senators, I didn't outwardly question or ridicule him for lying like I might have done with others, under such circumstances. I didn't even add a snarky comment, like I have done before.

Instead, I rose to my feet and went over to my Big Mac, open and ready for such an important occasion. I thought but didn't say out loud…*Let's just see if your name is in the book, Steve!* Sure enough, "Steve Korcheck" *was* in the book! He played from 1954 to 1959 as a catcher for the Washington Senators. He batted .159, coming to bat 145 times in 58 games. Most guys like me would have traded places with him in a heartbeat if given the chance. He wasn't an All-Star and didn't play on a World Series team, but he played Major League Baseball, and his name is in the book. That's more than most of us have done. Plus, they say he was a really nice guy and a good college president, so I was happy he wasn't a liar. No Eddie Scissons Syndrome Club for you, Dr. Korcheck!

Choosing principle over self-interest

It's always reassuring to hear that others have had similar experiences and similar reactions when encountering baseball imposters. My friend George Gmelch played minor league baseball and not just for the proverbial cup of coffee. George was a bona fide prospect in the Tigers organization, and had it not been for his outspoken objection to Jim Crow practices in the 1960s south, writing about his experiences in his hometown newspaper against the objection of Tigers management, he more than likely would be in the Big Mac today. George could have chosen to be silent, but he chose principle over career, and was released, ending his dream of a baseball career before ever reaching his potential. George then pursued a new path, achieving a highly successful academic career in Anthropology, teaching, writing, researching, and motivating hundreds if not thousands of students to pursue careers that improve the human condition.

George's gentle demeanor changes when he talks about encountering guys who tell him they also played minor league ball. He quizzes them about who, what, and where they played. "I can spot them right away!" he has told me. And then he settles down. It seems guys who have *earned* their valor are never pleased to see someone devalue it by misrepresenting themselves. And they think they can easily get away with these lies, until confronted by someone who has been there.

Chapter 20

BE PREPARED

We've spent the ensuing pages of the book covering Eddie Scissons Syndrome at length.

So, what do we do about it? As the late, legendary college football coach, Bill Peterson, once said when asked about the chance of rain for an upcoming big game, "How should I know, I'm not a geologist!"

Neither am I, but given my years of research on this topic, here are my suggestions:

Ask questions and take mental notes (or written notes, if possible).

Ask the so-called former big league ballplayer about the teammates they played with, their coaches, their favorite ballpark… ask them about their MLB debut, and look closely at them, notice how they respond. You can check out their eyes, give them that Larry David stare, see if they look away. Don't *you* look away, let them know you are paying attention to their response.

My friend George Gmelch has a great way of doing that. "Oh, really, you played for the Syracuse Chiefs? Is that right? "What year was that…? Who was managing the Chiefs then? Was it Frank Carswell? Bob Swift? Johnny Vander Meer? Was it Gene Verble?" "Was it Jewel Ens?" By now the guy is woozy. If he was a pitcher, ask who his pitching coach was. If he doesn't know that he's (*almost certainly*) a liar. If he says, "I think it was Carswell," you can follow up. "Oh, Carswell was managing then? So, what years did you say you played there? And what position did you play?" Keep asking questions until he breaks.

"Second base."

"So, you must remember Georgie Smith? And of course, Ray Oyler. Did you play with those guys?"

The more you know, the easier it is to ask follow-up questions, and to see for yourself he never played at triple-A Syracuse. If he's lying about being a former Syracuse Chief, well, he's probably lying about having played Major League Baseball too. Don't let him off the hook.

Just be curious and keep asking. You can make a mental note and research his answers later to see if what he told you matches up. If he really did play Major League Baseball, he might even pull up his Baseball Reference page or video clips of himself and show you some of his biggest moments. If he has reasonably good technical skills, that is.

It's probably best for your physical health and safety that you don't go around confronting people like I did with that chiropractor claiming he played for the Yankees. Things can get rather heated pretty fast, and at the present time there are no insurance policies available that are specifically designed for injuries sustained as a result of confronting those infected by the ESS virus.

Just ask questions and learn as much as you can. And take notes. Don't do anything foolish.

ACKNOWLEDGEMENTS

If, back in 1985, **Dr. Richard Crepeau** hadn't encouraged me to pursue the Eddie Scissons Syndrome phenomenon, I never would have pursued this body of knowledge, collected examples of cases, encouraged others to do the same, written and presented academic papers on this topic, and of course, I never would have written this book.

My friend Dick Crepeau saw something there, and as a respected college professor and mentor, he not only co-authored our first paper together on this subject just to help out a rookie like me but he gave me the green light to continue on this path, always motivating and encouraging me to move forward. And now, thanks to Professor Crepeau, together we have held hundreds of men accountable for their lies and discouraged thousands more from acting on the strange impulse to pass themselves off as former Major League Baseball players. As his many thousand former students know, Dr. Crepeau has made a difference in their lives through lessons taught and lectures presented in the classroom. And today we can say, Dick's pioneering work out in the field brings us closer to a cure.

After I presented what I thought would be the final word on this topic in a paper at the Cooperstown Symposium at the Baseball Hall of Fame in June 2023, (admittedly, the high point of my life), another highly respected college professor, writer of some pretty terrific baseball books, and a valued friend, **James Walker** came up to me and suggested I write a book on this subject. I laughed. It hadn't occurred to me there was more to say on this matter until my wife and I returned to our home in Florida several months later, and I was able to consult the file cabinet full of ESS stuff I had amassed over the years. It was becoming a fire hazard and needed to be cleaned out anyway before OSHA shut us down.

Jim Walker's encouragement meant a lot to me. I often wondered if this topic had such narrow appeal that I surely have taken it as far as it could go. Maybe I should just be content that the hundred or so audience members still at the conference, apparently with nowhere else to be, politely expressed their approval rather than laughing me off the stage at the Baseball Hall of Fame. Maybe that should be enough. But what about future generations, innocent victims, and what about finding a cure for this Syndrome?

Jim and his wife, Judith Hiltner wrote the award winning biography on Red Barber, among other brilliantly written baseball books, and his opinion carried a lot of weight.

The file cabinet contained personal notes and newspaper articles, postcards, letters, copies of emails and pictures of ESS victims sent to me from people I briefly encountered along the way. They contained cassette tapes with valuable interviews, a VHS tape but no machine capable of showing it anymore, articles from local and national newspapers and magazines, and correspondence from friends, some of whom were no longer living. Every time I gave a presentation, it seemed I was asked to cut it down further to fit the audience and leave some good stuff on the cutting-room floor.

And there was a lot of good stuff left on the cutting-room floor, ready to be unearthed one more time. And even as I organized my old scraps of paper collected over the years, current periodic news stories gave me new cases, friends shared anecdotes about a topic in which they knew I had interest. Fresh ones seemed to pop up almost daily in the news, worthy of investigation.

Jim Walker was right, and I was convinced, there was more to say about Eddie Scissons Syndrome. Thanks for that push, Jim. And of course, we're doing this for the kids.

Cassidy Lent, Director of the Library at the Baseball Hall of Fame, sent me the HOF electronic file on what they call "Phantom Players" which provided many new avenues for research. While they were more focused on players who nearly made it to the Bigs (Phantom Players) rather than liars who falsely claimed they had, there were many new eye-opening cases and some I had overlooked before, worthy of our attention. It seems Cassidy Lent is a name that pops up in the Acknowledgements of many books with a baseball theme for a good reason. She is a competent, generous, and dependable source of information for baseball researchers and her contribution cannot be recognized enough for expanding the body of knowledge in all aspects of baseball research.

Tim Wiles, retired Director of Research at the Baseball Hall of Fame, readily shared his time and advice, offering insights from his 20 years' experience at the Hall of Fame with numerous responsibilities, including responding to wives, sons and daughters, grandchildren and others inquiring about a deceased loved one who never played Major League baseball. That's a tough assignment and Tim Wiles always handled it with dignity and compassion for the families involved. I appreciate Tim sharing some of those experiences.

Fellow SABR member, **Bill Hickman** shared his time and insights, drawing on his many years doing research on Near Major Leaguers and Phantom Players. It was during my conversation with Bill that I discovered my naive use of the Phantom Players terminology and how it was different from his. This changed the course of direction for my research. Seeing the commitment he has for maintaining an accurate Phantom Players file, and the compassion he has for Phantom Players themselves helped me understand that Eddie Scissons Syndrome victims should not be confused with Phantom Players. ESS sufferers are liars, plain and simple. Phantom Players are baseball players, near major leaguers who worked their way up the minor league ladder, and had things gone just a little differently, had they avoided an injury or not been traded at just the wrong moment, had their timing been just a little better, they might have been entered into the Baseball Encyclopedia. Bill is right, these guys deserve our compassion and our respect, and he convinced me that I needed a new title for my book that more accurately portrayed the difference between these two categories. I appreciate his guidance and admire his dedication to this project on behalf of SABR.

George Gmelch played minor league baseball in the 1960's, and his award winning book "Playing with Tigers" documents his experience as well as the struggle of Black players on his team who had to find alternate housing, dining, and recreation outlets from their white teammates. George chose a humanitarian principle over his own personal gain, and after being released by the Tigers for exposing the injustice he saw first-hand in the Jim

Crowe South as a minor leaguer, he pursued a new path, finishing his education and earning a PhD, achieving a highly successful academic career in Anthropology, teaching, writing, researching, and motivating hundreds if not thousands of students to pursue careers that improve the human condition. His ability to inspire and motivate is not limited to his students, his encouragement as a friend kept me focused on bringing this project to completion, and I am grateful for that.

At the Sport Literature Association national conference in Florence, Oregon in 1990, I had the great privilege of playing a game of catch with **W.P. Kinsella**. I still have that old beat up baseball, which he signed "Go the Distance, Bill Kinsella" (proving the old adage that bringing a ball and glove with you wherever you go is always a good idea.) It was a memorable experience and led to a valuable conversation for this nascent researcher. Kinsella's story about the creation of the Eddie Scissons character for his book was reassuring and showed Dick Crepeau and me that we are not alone.

Hillary Clinton was right, it does take a village. So many people helped me make this final effort to tell the Eddie Scissons Syndrome story that I would be remiss if I didn't mention and thank them here and now.

Without **Dan Good's** professional editing and insightful, critical yet encouraging conversations, without his advice and expertise, I would have never been able to get this far in telling our story.

Joey Green's calm demeanor and wealth of experience in life and in book writing helped bring together and make sense of 40 years of notes and articles, from pre-Internet days when conversations were held through U.S. Mail, or on a telephone land line, with follow-up notes on pages of legal pads and lots of little yellow Post-it notes. Thanks to Joey I was able to see an organized sense of direction.

Graphic artist **Andy Meahan** created the book cover and the fake baseball cards, not bad for a guy who lives in rural England where baseball isn't played and certainly doesn't get much (any) press. Andy doesn't know if the ball is filled with air or water, but this guy has the patience of a saint. Working with me is not easy.

And **Kiersten Armstrong** has a knack for quietly getting things done; she is more than a talented Web designer with great technical and creative skills. Kiersten is someone who takes initiative to do what needs to be done and finds solutions to problems. I can't thank Kiersten enough for formatting the manuscript and bringing this project to completion.

Finally, I want to thank **Joseph Edward Cavallo**, (not his real name). If he hadn't brazenly, even creatively lied to me (for at least 4 or 5 continuous hours!) during our interview for my master's thesis back in the early 1980's, I never would have developed this obsession for what came to be known as Baseball Imposters. As Patient Zero, Joe Cavallo set the tone for others to follow. His bold lies were high profile enough to warrant a full scale investigation. And unlike Ray Kinsella in Field of Dreams, I did confront the guy. Sadly, the outcome of that confrontation was not satisfying, as is often the case when confronting an ESS liar, but give me credit… I exercised great restraint, I did not inform the authorities, (because I knew they wouldn't care). Had I called the police, I might have been arrested, or they might be amused, probably annoyed…because really, did Joe break any laws? Maybe not, but shame on him anyway. He got me started on this path, so I guess I should be thankful. And while he compromised my master's thesis, no one seemed to care, not even the academic department that conferred the degree. So, maybe I should just let it go? But if you know me, you know that probably won't happen and it has given me something to complain about for the past 40 years.

With this book complete, I intend to hand off the baton to a younger generation of ESS Busters. Godspeed to this new generation of researchers in bringing this epidemic under control, so future volumes of books like Baseball Imposters will not have to be written.

I'm grateful to the readers of this book, those who might find this subject of interest. There are a lot of sports books to choose from, and you chose this wacky topic over a biography of Clete Boyer or Ray Oyler, or Lefty O'Doul, or a discussion of the 1994 pennant race. I hope you have no regrets about that decision. And… good for you! (You can always go back to Clete and Lefty later on, those books will still be there.) Thank you for reading, I suspect some of these stories made you remember someone who told you he played Major League Baseball, and you readily believed him because you wanted to and had no reason to doubt him… but you failed to fact-check him back then even though something just didn't feel right about that conversation, and now you're wondering…. See? This is what I'm talking about!

If you'd like to keep the conversation going, please share your brush with Eddie Scissons Syndrome on my blog… visit our website and share your story for everyone to see at RobSheinkopf-author. com. Judging by the stories I hear at book signings and almost every time I read an excerpt from this book, your story will be in good company. You are not alone.

EPILOGUE

As I was putting the finishing touches on a manuscript to be delivered to the publisher of this book, I was forced to delay my progress in favor of a long planned cruise, along with eight members of my wife's family.

While off the coast of Malta, Lisa found the perfect use for my book, *Hey Mom, Wanna Have a Catch?* by using it to reserve a chair at the pool on board the ship. (I had it with me only because I was donating it to the ship's library, where I know it will surely become worn out and dog-eared in short order because we all know passengers on cruise ships just love books like that. Uh huh, they sure do).

As I approached our *reserved* chairs, I saw a guy standing over them, reading my book. He finally looked up. "Is this your book?" he asked.

"Well, yes it is," I replied. He then asked if it was a good book, whereupon I told him it was "*my* book," and then he got it. "Oh, you *wrote* this book?" Then he said, "I used to play for the Detroit Tigers."

Here we go again! I thought, "We're halfway around the world, and here is yet another case of Eddie Scissons Syndrome!" The rest of our conversation went as you might expect. He couldn't remember who the manager of the Tigers was when he played. I had to provide some names, and finally when I mentioned Les Moss, he said *he thought* that might have been right. What player doesn't know the name of the manager he played for? When I asked about who he played with, he responded by naming about five guys from different eras of the Tigers, all well-known by even casual baseball fans (Al Kaline, Norm Cash, Gates Brown, Denny McLain… I was surprised he didn't mention Ty Cobb or Hank Greenberg). He proudly told me he was from Detroit (probably why he knew all the names of all those Tigers), and "what a thrill it was playing for my hometown fans. They really treated us well." When I asked what minor league teams he played for, he mumbled something about "Indianapolis, and maybe Columbus, I'm not sure." I told him I grew up in Syracuse, a triple-A affiliate of the Tigers in the 60's and he said he had played there, but not very convincingly. He got more uneasy as the *interrogation* went on, and finally moved on (probably to tell more lies to someone else, somewhere else, about something else).

I looked him up as soon as the ship's sporadic Wi-Fi kicked in, and of course his name was nowhere to be seen anywhere. I'm sure he thought …*We're on a cruise ship, miles from anyone who knows me, I'll never see this guy again, and he looks like he'd believe anything. So, what the hell? Why not tell him I had played for the Detroit Tigers? Feels good being a former Big Leaguer! I almost believe it myself…*

Sadly, the conversation ended on an even more sour note. After he told me he plays in Old-Timers games and keeps in touch with many of his former teammates quite often, he mentioned a few former Tigers by name. "*Why, I just heard from my buddy, Bill Freehan a couple weeks ago… I was his* (wait for it), *back-up catcher!*"

Never mind that Freehan died in 2021 at the age of 79.

You'll buy this book, if you know what's good for you.